Paolo Ben Salmi aka Pint

PINT SIZE ADVENTURER

\-

MINDSET IS

KEY

Paolo Ben Salmi aka Pint Size Adventurer

UK Ambassadors of the Borg Banking Group AND of Borg University of International Skills, Award Winning Author, US Africa Chamber Youth Ambassador to Global Diaspora United Voices for Economic Empowerment Forum & Ambassador for Water-to-Go, founded Sarva Education, VueBox, TruChallenge & Choose Love

Paolo Ben Salmi aka Pint Size Adventurer

ADVENTUROUS
PUBLISHING

PUBLISHER
Adventurous Publishing

ISBN: 978-1-913310-33-2

DEDICATION

This book is dedicated to you.

I also want to dedicate this book to my mum and dad
Sabrina Ben Salmi aka Dura Mater and Mohammed Ben Salmi.
My sister Lashai Ben Salmi aka Dreampreneur, brother
Tray-Sean Ben Salmi aka I'm That KID & Child Genius Advisor,
sister Yasmine Ben Salmi aka Lovepreneur, brother Amire Ben
Salmi aka Mr Intelligent, Mary Paul my Nan and founder of Mary
Pauls Creations, and Style Me Happy. My Abuelo Alan Shelton &
Abuela Justine Shelton www.alanshelton.com

ACKNOWLEDGMENTS

I would like to thank all of my family and friends for being in my
life.

I would like to express my deepest appreciation to Robert Vilkelis
for helping me to extract the key teachings from the chapters of my
book called "Pint Size Adventurer - 10 Key Principles To Get Your
KIDs of Their iPad and Into The Wild" which led to the creation of
my 3-step system called "The Abundant Adventure Creator".

I would also like to express my deepest appreciation to Sunil
Chunni via Virgin Money Lounge, Carl Southwell & James
MacDonald via Chelsea FC Foundation for sponsoring my
workshops. I would like to convey my appreciation to Lesley Warren
and the entire STEM team via Brunel University. I would like to
convey my appreciation to Regan Hillyer & Juanpa Barahona. I
would like to give my appreciation to Shadia Daho, Jaadin Daho aka
JD The Kid & Arabella Daho aka Amazing Arabella. I would also
like to thank Pete Craig & Daniel Wagner co-founders of Simply
Conscious for inviting me and my mum to join the Wisdom Council
and for making us (me, Lashai, Tray-Sean, Yasmine, Amire, Daniel
Barahona & Abuelo Alan Shelton) founding members of Simply
Conscious Next Generation. Which became Sarva Education next
generation education turning learners into leaders. I would also like
to thank Travis Fox founder of The Architects of Being. I would like
to thank Anoir Houmou founder of VueBox for selecting me to be
one of his brand ambassadors. I would also like to thank Tim Chase
founder of TruChallenge for making me an ambassador for his
company. A huge thank you to Malik Muhammad founder of
www.malikmuhammad.com and Ben Green founder of
www.activ8tion.co.uk. I would like to thank members from our
Diaspora mastermind group: founder Sir Joe Madu (thank you s
much for all of your wisdom and guidance Sir Joe) & Priscilla Madu
(thank you so much for all of your prays and encouragement auntie
Priscilla). Dr Toby Bailey aka Abba Borg, Quintus McDonald,
Captin Kerry Grant, Lola Odujinrin, HE Amb Arikana Chihombori

Quao, Sir Dr Joe Madu, Prof. Chimezie, Dr Debbie Bartlett, HE Amb.(Rtd) Robert Perry, Robert Barnard-Weston, Col Brian Searcy (Rtd-USAF), Lamido Umar, Keston White-Marin, Evelyn Okpanachi, Briony Vanden Bussche, Prof. Abraham Osinubi, Alison Hall, Gunter Pauli, Steven Fern, Kanayo O. Kanayo, Hon. Kizito Ikenna. Our Abuelo Alan Shelton & Abuela Justine Shelton for being oak trees in our lives. I value and appreciate Denise Ramsey via UnLtd for all of her support and encouragement to date. Our SoulJah Kingdon Rise family Winston Hislop, Rasheda Ashanti Malcolm, Rasher B McNeish and Zabdiel Campbell for bringing Kingdom to life. Apostle Linda Edwards for all your prays. Rev Dr Trevor Adams for your commitment and support.

CONTENT

INTRODUCTION

There was a time in my life when I use to feel bored, empty, disconnected, angry, lonely and scared of being rejected. I did not know how to keep my mind occupied.

As I grew through life by immersing myself into a life of personal development. In life I believe that there are two types of journeys that we can go on, a journey of self-discovery and one outdoors in the wild. I also believe that in order to embark on a journey of self-discovery it would need to begin with WHY!

My mindset began to shift, and I began to observe life with an entirely new perspective.

My commitment to follow this calling grew and, in the process, a divine intelligence came into my life and softly guided me in my life journey.

This is when I created my three-step system with the help of Robert Vilkelis called "The Abundant Adventure creator™" which aims to inspire people to become RESPONSIBLE, MANAGE themselves better and allow themselves to EXPRESS themselves more. Here's an example of my 3-step system.

#1 RESPONSIBILITY
"The Real Life REEL™" which focuses on the choices that we always have in life because I believe that we can watch the movie, be in the movie, direct the movie or you can produce the movie.

#2 MANAGEMENT
"Mystic MAP Maker™" which focuses on developing positive habitual actions, how to participate in high vibration activities, how to deal with interruptions that will show up in life and how timing is everything.

#3 EXPRESSION
"Rise and Shine™" which delves into the importance of reading, interests, socialising and internal and external exploration.

21 MINDSET RE-SET – NOW INSIGHTS

#1 INNER COMPASS

Shifting my mindset to self-belief, surrendering and trusting my intuition, that was the difference that made the difference
Mindset-Reset Now!

RESPONSIBILITY

When you shift your mindset to self-belief, surrender to the process and trust your intuition that will be the difference that will make the difference. I believe that you should take full responsibility in your life instead of giving your power away by running around aimlessly in life like sheeple. It is time to STEP into your POWER right here and right now. It is your divine birth right sovereignty to action your freewill and create your desired lifestyle. *You can either watch the movie, be in the movie, direct the movie or you can produce the movie.*

MANAGEMENT

When you shift your mindset to self-belief, surrender to the process and trust your intuition that will be the difference that will make the difference. You are the CEO of your life. *In life you are not defined by the things that happen to you, what matters most is how you choose to respond to the contrast that shows up in your life and that starts with having a fertile mindset.*

EXPRESSION

When you shift your mindset to self-belief, surrender to the process and trust your intuition that will be the difference that will make the difference. Being able to express yourself is key for your positive development. *I believe that our emotions are merely our internal guidance system therefore when we give ourselves permission to express ourselves we are choosing to honour and accept all parts of us and that includes our so-called shadow self.*

DAILY MANTRA
"Stop using a compass your entire life, because your true compass is inside of you and it is your heart." Paolo Ben Salmi

#2 YOU ARE RIGHT

When I came to realise that whether I think I can, or whether I think I can't, I am right. Therefore, giving myself permission to believe in myself more often seemed like a plausible choice. *Mindset-Reset Now!*

RESPONSIBILITY

When you come to realise that whether you think you can, or whether you think you can't, YOU ARE RIGHT. Therefore, giving yourself permission to believe in yourself more often seems like a plausible choice. I believe that it is your responsibility to become your own best friend and in doing so I truly believe that you will become the best version of you. *You can either watch the movie, be in the movie, direct the movie or you can produce the movie.*

MANAGEMENT

When you come to realise that whether you think you can, or whether you think you can't, YOU ARE RIGHT. Therefore, giving yourself permission to believe in yourself more often seems like a plausible choice. Learning to manage your life from a place of self-reflection sounds like a good starting place for you to manage yourself in the best possible way. *In life you are not defined by the things that happen to you, what matters most is how you choose to respond to the contrast that shows up in your life and that starts with having a fertile mindset.*

EXPRESSION

When you come to realise that whether you think you can, or whether you think you can't, YOU ARE RIGHT. Therefore, giving yourself permission to believe in yourself more often seems like a plausible choice. Being able to express yourself is key for your positive development. *I believe that our emotions are merely our internal guidance system therefore when we give ourselves permission to express ourselves we are choosing to honour and accept all parts of us and that includes our so-called shadow self.*

DAILY MANTRA

"Whether you think you can, or you think you can't - you're right." Henry Ford

#3 SURRENDER

When I came to realise the fact that no one said it'll be easy; however, it'll be worth it – so I chose to enjoy the journey and just surrender.
Mindset-Reset Now!

RESPONSIBILITY

When you shift your mindset and realise the fact that no one said it'll be easy; however, it'll be worth it. You can choose to enjoy the journey and just surrender. I believe that you should take responsibility when it comes to letting go and simply enjoying the journey by surrendering to the process. *You can either watch the movie, be in the movie, direct the movie or you can produce the movie.*

MANAGEMENT

When you shift your mindset and realise the fact that no one said it'll be easy; however, it'll be worth it. You can choose to enjoy the journey and just surrender. Managing your mindset is the difference that'll make the difference in all areas of your life. *In life you are not defined by the things that happen to you, what matters most is how you choose to respond to the contrast that shows up in your life and that starts with having a fertile mindset.*

EXPRESSION

When you shift your mindset and realise the fact that no one said it'll be easy; however, it'll be worth it. You can choose to enjoy the journey and just surrender. Self-expression will become a habitual action. *I believe that our emotions are merely our internal guidance system therefore when we give ourselves permission to express ourselves we are choosing to honour and accept all parts of us and that includes our so-called shadow self.*

DAILY MANTRA
"No one said it'll be easy; however, I can say that it'll be worth it – enjoy the journey and surrender." Paolo Ben Salmi

#4 YOU BECOME WHAT YOU THINK OF MOST

When I came to realise that my mind is everything. What I think, I
become.
Mindset-Reset Now!

RESPONSIBILITY

*When you shift your mindset to the realisation that your mind is everything.
What you think, you will become.* I encourage you to take responsibility
for the words that you say to yourself because you are the first
person to hear them. *You can either watch the movie, be in the movie, direct
the movie or you can produce the movie.*

MANAGEMENT

*When you shift your mindset to the realisation that your mind is everything.
What you think, you will become.* Managing your thoughts will empower
you to create the life you deserve. *In life you are not defined by the things
that happen to you, what matters most is how you choose to respond to the contrast
that shows up in your life and that starts with having a fertile mindset.*

EXPRESSION

*When you shift your mindset to the realisation that your mind is everything.
What you think, you will become.* Having thoughts of your desired
outcomes will inspire you to express yourself in a more authentic
way. *I believe that our emotions are merely our internal guidance system therefore
when we give ourselves permission to express ourselves we are choosing to honour
and accept all parts of us and that includes our so-called shadow self.*

DAILY MANTRA
"The mind is everything. What you think, you become." Buddha

#5 BE KIND

When I shifted my mindset to being kind, after realising the fact that everyone I meet is fighting a hard battle.
Mindset-Reset Now!

RESPONSIBILITY

When you choose to shift your mindset to being kind, you'll come to realise that everyone you meet is fighting a hard battle. How others treat you reflects their character, just because someone is unkind towards you does not mean that you have to do the same. I encourage you to take responsible to be care to those around you. *You can either watch the movie, be in the movie, direct the movie or you can produce the movie.*

MANAGEMENT

When you choose to shift your mindset to being kind, you'll come to realise that everyone you meet is fighting a hard battle. Self-management sets you free. *In life you are not defined by the things that happen to you, what matters most is how you choose to respond to the contrast that shows up in your life and that starts with having a fertile mindset.*

EXPRESSION

When you choose to shift your mindset to being kind, you'll come to realise that everyone you meet is fighting a hard battle. Being able to express yourself in a kind way is absolute paramount. *I believe that our emotions are merely our internal guidance system therefore when we give ourselves permission to express ourselves we are choosing to honour and accept all parts of us and that includes our so-called shadow self.*

DAILY MANTRA
"Be kind, for everyone you meet is fighting a hard battle." Socrates

#6 PLANT A SEED

When I came to the realisation that the creation of a thousand forests is in one acorn, that was the difference that made the difference.
Mindset-Reset Now!

RESPONSIBILITY

When you shift your mindset to the realisation that the creation of a thousand forests is in one acorn, that will be the difference that will make the difference. Inside of you is the seed that houses a thousand possibilities, please do not let your dreams die inside of you – you have the responsibility to share your dreams with the world. *You can either watch the movie, be in the movie, direct the movie or you can produce the movie.*

MANAGEMENT

When you shift your mindset to the realisation that the creation of a thousand forests is in one acorn, that will be the difference that will make the difference. I believe that when you give yourself permission to better manage and share the true potency of the unique essence that is deep within you. That is the moment that you will truly plant your seed within this lifetime. *In life you are not defined by the things that happen to you, what matters most is how you choose to respond to the contrast that shows up in your life and that starts with having a fertile mindset.*

EXPRESSION

When you shift your mindset to the realisation that the creation of a thousand forests is in one acorn, that will be the difference that will make the difference. You are the seed that creation desired to plant within this would and yourself express is your gift to the world. *I believe that our emotions are merely our internal guidance system therefore when we give ourselves permission to express ourselves we are choosing to honour and accept all parts of us and that includes our so-called shadow self.*

DAILY MANTRA
"The creation of a thousand forests is in one acorn." Ralph Waldo Emerson

#7 PEACE

When I shifted my mindset to the realisation of the fact that peace comes from within and not to seek it without – it was a game changer.
Mindset-Reset Now!

RESPONSIBILITY

When you shift your mindset to the realisation of the fact that peace comes from within and not to seek it without – it'll be a game changer. Take responsibility to first seek within and do not define yourself by other people's standards. *You can either watch the movie, be in the movie, direct the movie or you can produce the movie.*

MANAGEMENT

When you shift your mindset to the realisation of the fact that peace comes from within and not to seek it without – it'll be a game changer. Managing how the opinions of others impact you is the key to true freedom. *In life you are not defined by the things that happen to you, what matters most is how you choose to respond to the contrast that shows up in your life and that starts with having a fertile mindset.*

EXPRESSION

When you shift your mindset to the realisation of the fact that peace comes from within and not to seek it without – it'll be a game changer. Your ability to express yourself will improve as a direct result of surrendering to this new reality. *I believe that our emotions are merely our internal guidance system therefore when we give ourselves permission to express ourselves we are choosing to honour and accept all parts of us and that includes our so-called shadow self.*

DAILY MANTRA
"Peace comes from within. Do not seek it without." Buddha

#8 YOUR OWN MIND

When I came to comprehend the fact that it is a man's own mind
not his enemy or foe, that lures him to evil ways. This expanded
my awareness of my innate power in a deeply profound way.
Mindset-Reset Now!

RESPONSIBILITY

*When you choose to comprehend the fact that it is a man's own mind not his
enemy or foe, that lures him to evil ways. This will expand your awareness of
your innate power in a deeply profound way.* It is your responsibility to give
yourself permission to reclaim your inner ability/sovereign birth
right and set yourself FREE now. *You can either watch the movie, be in
the movie, direct the movie or you can produce the movie.*

MANAGEMENT

*When you choose to comprehend the fact that it is a man's own mind not his
enemy or foe, that lures him to evil ways. This will expand your awareness of
your innate power in a deeply profound way.* This new shift in mindset could
grant you the opportunity to manage your life in a deeply profound
way. Learn to manage your emotions, forgive and let go. *In life you are
not defined by the things that happen to you, what matters most is how you choose
to respond to the contrast that shows up in your life and that starts with having
a fertile mindset.*

EXPRESSION

*When you choose to comprehend the fact that it is a man's own mind not his
enemy or foe, that lures him to evil ways. This will expand your awareness of
your innate power in a deeply profound way.* This NEW mindset shift can
grant you a new opportunity to express yourself in a deeper way. *I
believe that our emotions are merely our internal guidance system therefore when
we give ourselves permission to express ourselves we are choosing to honour and
accept all parts of us and that includes our so-called shadow self.*

DAILY MANTRA
"It is a man's own mind not his enemy or foe, that lures him to evil ways." Buddha

#9 YOUR ARE THE AUTHOR OF YOUR LIFE

When I learned that the BEST way to predict the future is to create it. I totally began to see life with a new perspective.
Mindset-Reset Now!

RESPONSIBILITY

When you learn that the BEST way to predict the future is to create it. You will totally begin to see life with a new perspective. Taking responsibility for manifesting your desired lifestyle, it will give you a deep sense of fulfilment. *You can either watch the movie, be in the movie, direct the movie or you can produce the movie.*

MANAGEMENT

When you learn that the BEST way to predict the future is to create it. You will totally begin to see life with a new perspective. When you manage your life by actively crafting your future – the true essence of creation will activate and in this very moment all things are possible. *In life you are not defined by the things that happen to you, what matters most is how you choose to respond to the contrast that shows up in your life and that starts with having a fertile mindset.*

EXPRESSION

When you learn that the BEST way to predict the future is to create it. You will totally begin to see life with a new perspective. Your essence of self-expression will begin to amplify in ways that will totally blow your mind. *I believe that our emotions are merely our internal guidance system therefore when we give ourselves permission to express ourselves we are choosing to honour and accept all parts of us and that includes our so-called shadow self.*

DAILY MANTRA
"The BEST way to predict the future is to create it." Abraham Lincoln

#10 PAY IT FORWARD

When I began to understand that happiness never decreases by being shared. I began to embrace the sacred gift of paying it forward.
Mindset-Reset Now!

RESPONSIBILITY

When you begin to understand that happiness never decreases by being shared. You will begin to embrace the sacred gift of GIVING/PAYING IT FORWARD. Sharing is caring and when we tap into the sacred essence of giving and receiving life becomes super exciting. *You can either watch the movie, be in the movie, direct the movie or you can produce the movie.*

MANAGEMENT

When you begin to understand that happiness never decreases by being shared. You will begin to embrace the sacred gift of GIVING/PAYING IT FORWARD. You've got this, and I believe in you. Learn to positively manage your life or your life will manage you. *In life you are not defined by the things that happen to you, what matters most is how you choose to respond to the contrast that shows up in your life and that starts with having a fertile mindset.*

EXPRESSION

When you begin to understand that happiness never decreases by being shared. You will begin to embrace the sacred gift of GIVING/PAYING IT FORWARD. The more you give, the more you will free yourself to fully express yourself though the art of giving. *I believe that our emotions are merely our internal guidance system therefore when we give ourselves permission to express ourselves we are choosing to honour and accept all parts of us and that includes our so-called shadow self.*

DAILY MANTRA
"Happiness never decreases by being shared." Buddha

#11 LAYING THE FOUNDATION

When I learned that the beginning is the most important part of
the work, I grew to realise that the foundation sets the tone for
future developments.
Mindset-Reset Now!

RESPONSIBILITY

*When I learned that the beginning is the most important part of the work, I grew
to realise that the foundation sets the tone for future developments.* I believe
that you should take full responsibility in your life instead of giving
your power away by running around aimlessly in life like other
sheeple. It is time to STEP into your POWER which is your divine
birth right sovereignty to action your freewill and create your desired
lifestyle. *You can either watch the movie, be in the movie, direct the movie or
you can produce the movie.*

MANAGEMENT

*When you shift your mindset to self-belief, surrender to the process and trust your
intuition that will be the difference that will make the difference.* You are the
CEO of your life. *In life you are not defined by the things that happen to you,
what matters most is how you choose to respond to the contrast that shows up in
your life and that starts with having a fertile mindset.*

EXPRESSION

*When you shift your mindset to self-belief, surrender to the process and trust your
intuition that will be the difference that will make the difference.* Being able to
express yourself is key for your positive development. *I believe that our
emotions are merely our internal guidance system therefore when we give ourselves
permission to express ourselves we are choosing to honour and accept all parts of
us and that includes our so-called shadow self.*

DAILY MANTRA
"The beginning is the most important part of the work." Plato

#12 FRIENDSHIP IS PRICELESS

When I came to the realisation that there is nothing on this earth
more to be prized than true friendship. I began to deeply
appreciate the friendships in my life.
Mindset-Reset Now!

RESPONSIBILITY

*When you come to the realisation that there is nothing on this earth more to be
prized than true friendship. You will begin to deeply appreciate the friendships
that you have in your life.* Take responsibility for your friendships by
cherishing them for a lifetime because these bonds are sacred. *You
can either watch the movie, be in the movie, direct the movie or you can produce
the movie.*

MANAGEMENT

*When you come to the realisation that there is nothing on this earth more to be
prized than true friendship. You will begin to deeply appreciate the friendships
that you have in your life.* When you begin to manage the array of
friendships in your life, you will grow to learn the importance of
contextual relationships. This will assist you to discover the true
friendships that you are blessed to have in your life. *In life you are not
defined by the things that happen to you, what matters most is how you choose to
respond to the contrast that shows up in your life and that starts with having a
fertile mindset.*

EXPRESSION

*When you come to the realisation that there is nothing on this earth more to be
prized than true friendship. You will begin to deeply appreciate the friendships
that you have in your life.* When you grow to learn to cherish friendships,
this will enable you to create a sacred space for you both to express
yourselves at a deeper level beyond your current awareness. *I believe
that our emotions are merely our internal guidance system therefore when we give
ourselves permission to express ourselves we are choosing to honour and accept all
parts of us and that includes our so-called shadow self.*

DAILY MANTRA
"There is nothing on this earth more to be prized than true friendship." St. Thomas Aquinas

#13 NECTAR

When I began to comprehend the fact that LIFE is the flower for which love is the honey. This was the difference that made the difference.
Mindset-Reset Now!

RESPONSIBILITY

When you began to comprehend the fact that LIFE is the flower for which love is the honey. This will be the difference that will make the difference. It is your responsibility to allow yourself to fully experience the sweet nectar that life has to offer. *You can either watch the movie, be in the movie, direct the movie or you can produce the movie.*

MANAGEMENT

When you began to comprehend the fact that LIFE is the flower for which love is the honey. This will be the difference that will make the difference. Learning to manage the sweet nectar in life has the power to yield you huge benefits. *In life you are not defined by the things that happen to you, what matters most is how you choose to respond to the contrast that shows up in your life and that starts with having a fertile mindset.*

EXPRESSION

When you began to comprehend the fact that LIFE is the flower for which love is the honey. This will be the difference that will make the difference. The sweet nectar of life can empower you to fully express yourself in the most effortless way. *I believe that our emotions are merely our internal guidance system therefore when we give ourselves permission to express ourselves we are choosing to honour and accept all parts of us and that includes our so-called shadow self.*

DAILY MANTRA
"Life is the flower for which love is the honey." Victor Hugo

#14 IMAGINE THE POSSIBILITIES

When I came to realise that I could choose to Imagine the possibilities, that was the difference that made the difference
Mindset-Reset Now!

RESPONSIBILITY

When you come to realise that you can choose to Imagine the possibilities, that will be the difference that makes the difference. Take responsibility to become the CEO of your mind, so much so that you develop a laser beam focus and grant yourself permission to imagine an abundance of possibilities. *You can either watch the movie, be in the movie, direct the movie or you can produce the movie.*

MANAGEMENT

When you come to realise that you can choose to Imagine the possibilities, that will be the difference that makes the difference. Manage your mindset and you will totally transform the way you perceive life. *In life you are not defined by the things that happen to you, what matters most is how you choose to respond to the contrast that shows up in your life and that starts with having a fertile mindset*

EXPRESSION

When you come to realise that you can choose to Imagine the possibilities, that will be the difference that makes the difference. Your ability to set yourself no matter how things may appear to be, will grant you a deep sense of free of self-expression. *I believe that our emotions are merely our internal guidance system therefore when we give ourselves permission to express ourselves we are choosing to honour and accept all parts of us and that includes our so-called shadow self.*

DAILY MANTRA

"Imagine the possibilities." Dr Toby Bailey aka Abba Borg

#15 CLOSING THE GENERATIONAL GAP

When I came to realise the importance of closing the generational
gap by way of having meaningful conversations and being
committed to developing lifelong relationships ranging from 0-100.
I became inspired to hand the baton to the next generation as it'll
empower them for eternity. This was a game changer for me.
Mindset-Reset Now!

RESPONSIBILITY

*When you come to realise the importance of closing the generational gap by way
of having meaningful conversations and being committed to developing lifelong
relationships ranging from 0-100. You will become inspired to hand the baton
to the next generation as it'll empower them for eternity. This will be a game
changer for you.* I truly believe that it is our responsibility today to do,
be and have the very best to our capability to make it easier for the
next generation to run their relay. When we transfer wisdom to those
around us we can totally transform the trajectory of a nation for
generations to come. *You can either watch the movie, be in the movie, direct
the movie or you can produce the movie.*

MANAGEMENT

*When you come to realise the importance of closing the generational gap by way
of having meaningful conversations and being committed to developing lifelong
relationships ranging from 0-100. You will become inspired to hand the baton
to the next generation as it'll empower them for eternity. This will be a game
changer for you.* when you grow to take this seriously you totally
transform the way you manage your life. *In life you are not defined by the
things that happen to you, what matters most is how you choose to respond to the
contrast that shows up in your life and that starts with having a fertile mindset.*

EXPRESSION

*When you come to realise the importance of closing the generational gap by way
of having meaningful conversations and being committed to developing lifelong
relationships ranging from 0-100. You will become inspired to hand the baton
to the next generation as it'll empower them for eternity. This will be a game*

changer for you. This level of realisation will empower you to become unapologetically your authentic self. *I believe that our emotions are merely our internal guidance system therefore when we give ourselves permission to express ourselves we are choosing to honour and accept all parts of us and that includes our so-called shadow self.*

DAILY MANTRA
"Closing the generational gap is key." Sir Joe Madu

#16 YOUR NETWORK

When I came to realise that my network is key to my success, I
became super excited about life.
Mindset-Reset Now!

RESPONSIBILITY

*When you come to realise that your network is key to your success, you will
become super excited about life.* Take responsibility to be of service to
your network. Help them to solve their problems. Learn to use
things and cherish people. These habits will aid you in developing
healthy habitual habits of behaviour. *You can either watch the movie, be
in the movie, direct the movie or you can produce the movie.*

MANAGEMENT

*When you come to realise that your network is key to your success, you will
become super excited about life.* The way you treat others will have a huge
impact on your internal and external world. *In life you are not defined by
the things that happen to you, what matters most is how you choose to respond to
the contrast that shows up in your life and that starts with having a fertile
mindset.*

EXPRESSION

*When you come to realise that your network is key to your success, you will
become super excited about life.* You will grow a deep sense of gratitude
and this will be felt by yourself and others in every essence of your
external and internal expression. *I believe that our emotions are merely our
internal guidance system therefore when we give ourselves permission to express
ourselves we are choosing to honour and accept all parts of us and that includes
our so-called shadow self.*

DAILY MANTRA
"Your network is key to your success." Quintus McDonald

#17 UNITY

When I came to realise the fact that together all things are possible,
life began to take on an entirely new meaning.
Mindset-Reset Now!

RESPONSIBILITY

*When you come to realise the fact that together all things are possible, life will
begin to take on an entirely new meaning.* It is in this moment that you will
begin to grasp the deeper meaning of the importance of unity,
because divided we fall and united all things are possible. Your life
is your responsibility. *You can either watch the movie, be in the movie, direct
the movie or you can produce the movie.*

MANAGEMENT

*When you come to realise the fact that together all things are possible, life will
begin to take on an entirely new meaning.* Shifting your perspective of life,
grants you a new opportunity to better manage yourself and life as it
organically unfolds. *In life you are not defined by the things that happen to
you, what matters most is how you choose to respond to the contrast that shows
up in your life and that starts with having a fertile mindset.*

EXPRESSION

*When you come to realise the fact that together all things are possible, life will
begin to take on an entirely new meaning.* The ability to express yourself is
the ultimate reward. *I believe that our emotions are merely our internal
guidance system therefore when we give ourselves permission to express ourselves
we are choosing to honour and accept all parts of us and that includes our so-
called shadow self.*

DAILY MANTRA
"Together all things are possible." HE Amb Robert Perry

#18 EMPOWERMENT

Coming to the realisation that leaders originate for others to imitate, makes me feel whole and complete.
Mindset-Reset Now!

RESPONSIBILITY

Coming to the realisation that leaders originate for others to imitate, can make you feel whole and complete. This knowledge can grant you the ability to gain a deep sense of responsibility for the way you create your lifestyle. When you give yourself permission to originate for others to imitate, it'll be a game changer that will set you FREE. *You can either watch the movie, be in the movie, direct the movie or you can produce the movie.*

MANAGEMENT

Coming to the realisation that leaders originate for others to imitate, can make you feel whole and complete. The way you manage your lifestyle will shift as a result of integrating this new sense of awareness into your life. *In life you are not defined by the things that happen to you, what matters most is how you choose to respond to the contrast that shows up in your life and that starts with having a fertile mindset.*

EXPRESSION

Coming to the realisation that leaders originate for others to imitate, can make you feel whole and complete. Your ability to express yourself will shift once this is immersed into your new expanded awareness. *I believe that our emotions are merely our internal guidance system therefore when we give ourselves permission to express ourselves we are choosing to honour and accept all parts of us and that includes our so-called shadow self.*

DAILY MANTRA
"Leaders originate for others to imitate " Malik Muhammad

#19 RENDERING THE STORY

When I learned how to remain connected to consciousness and allow my spiritual journey to happen through me. That was the moment that I granted myself permission to watch the story as it organically unfolds.
Mindset-Reset Now!

RESPONSIBILITY

When you learn how to remain connected to consciousness and allow your spiritual journey to happen through you, that'll be the moment that you grant yourself permission to watch the story as it organically unfolds. Taking responsibility to remain connected with your original story will empower you to observe yours and the stories of others in the world in a deeply profound way. *You can either watch the movie, be in the movie, direct the movie or you can produce the movie.*

MANAGEMENT

When you learn how to remain connected to consciousness and allow your spiritual journey to happen through you, that'll be the moment that you grant yourself permission to watch the story as it organically unfolds. This new expanded awareness of being in the choice can grant you opportunity to better manage your perception and how you respond to life from a place of love to that which shows up in your life. *In life you are not defined by the things that happen to you, what matters most is how you choose to respond to the contrast that shows up in your life and that starts with having a fertile mindset.*

EXPRESSION

When you learn how to remain connected to consciousness and allow your spiritual journey to happen through you, that'll be the moment that you grant yourself permission to watch the story as it organically unfolds. Giving yourself permission to fully express yourself from a place of authenticity can generate huge ripple effects of positivity. Your original story is the gateway to your soul and it can spark inspiration from your core and that will take you to a place that you can call home. *I believe that our emotions are merely our internal guidance system therefore when we give ourselves permission to express ourselves we are choosing to honour and accept all parts of us and that includes our so-called shadow self.*

DAILY MANTRA
"Remain connected to consciousness and allow your spiritual journey to happen through you." Alan Shelton aka Abuelo/Fiery Dragon

#20 INSERT HEALTHY BOUNDARIES

When I learned how to insert healthy boundaries into my life, I
began to feel more at ease with myself and others.
Mindset-Reset Now!

RESPONSIBILITY

When you learn how to insert healthy boundaries into your life, you will begin to feel more at ease with yourself and others. I believe that you should take full responsibility in your life instead of giving your power away by running around aimlessly in life like sheeple. It is time to STEP into your POWER which is your divine birth right sovereignty to action your freewill and create your desired lifestyle. *You can either watch the movie, be in the movie, direct the movie or you can produce the movie.*

MANAGEMENT

When you learn how to insert healthy boundaries into your life, you will begin to feel more at ease with yourself and others. Managing healthy boundaries within your life is the difference that'll make the difference in all areas of your life. *In life you are not defined by the things that happen to you, what matters most is how you choose to respond to the contrast that shows up in your life and that starts with having a fertile mindset.*

EXPRESSION

When you learn how to insert healthy boundaries into your life, you will begin to feel more at ease with yourself and others. This new expanded awareness can be the seed to an entirely new level of self-expression. *I believe that our emotions are merely our internal guidance system therefore when we give ourselves permission to express ourselves we are choosing to honour and accept all parts of us and that includes our so-called shadow self.*

DAILY MANTRA
"Insert healthy boundaries." Justine Shelton aka Abuela
Rainbow Butterfly

#21 ACTIV8TION

When I learned that Inspir8tion + Motiv8tion + Deadic8tion =
Activ8tion that was truly a heart-warming moment.
Mindset-Reset Now!

RESPONSIBILITY

When you learn that Inspir8tion + Motiv8tion + Deadic8tion = Activ8tion that can truly be a heart-warming moment. I believe that you should take full responsibility in your life instead of giving your power away by running around aimlessly in life like sheeple. It is time to STEP into your POWER which is your divine birth right sovereignty to action your freewill and create your desired lifestyle. *You can either watch the movie, be in the movie, direct the movie or you can produce the movie.*

MANAGEMENT

When you learn that Inspir8tion + Motiv8tion + Deadic8tion = Activ8tion that can truly be a heart-warming moment. This realisation grants you the opportunity to manage your life in a more profound way. *In life you are not defined by the things that happen to you, what matters most is how you choose to respond to the contrast that shows up in your life and that starts with having a fertile mindset.*

EXPRESSION

When you learn that Inspir8tion + Motiv8tion + Deadic8tion = Activ8tion that can truly be a heart-warming moment. Take a moment to observe how you will express yourself in a way that will totally blow your mind. *I believe that our emotions are merely our internal guidance system therefore when we give ourselves permission to express ourselves we are choosing to honour and accept all parts of us and that includes our so-called shadow self.*

DAILY MANTRA
"Inspir8tion + Motiv8tion + Deadic8tion = Activ8tion." Ben
Green

SURPRISE BONUS MINDSET PRINCIPLES

#22 YOU ARE THE SUBJECT

When I grew to understand that I am the subject in my life and that
all lessons are there to assist me to develop key disciplines. Just
knowing that all things are connected was such an awakening
moment for me.
Mindset-Reset Now!

RESPONSIBILITY

*When you grew to understand that you are the subject in your life and that all
lessons are there to assist you to develop key disciplines. Just knowing that all
things are connected can be such an awakening moment for you.* It is your
responsibility to seek knowledge that will empower you to grow. Just
know that everything is connected and that you are the main subject
in your life. *You can either watch the movie, be in the movie, direct the movie
or you can produce the movie.*

MANAGEMENT

*When you grew to understand that you are the subject in your life and that all
lessons are there to assist you to develop key disciplines. Just knowing that all
things are connected can be such an awakening moment for you.* This new
expanded awareness can grant you the ability to better manage
yourself and that which shows up in your life. *In life you are not defined
by the things that happen to you, what matters most is how you choose to respond
to the contrast that shows up in your life and that starts with having a fertile
mindset.*

EXPRESSION

*When you grew to understand that you are the subject in your life and that all
lessons are there to assist you to develop key disciplines. Just knowing that all
things are connected can be such an awakening moment for you.* This new shift
in awareness will transform the way you express yourself both
internally and externally. *I believe that our emotions are merely our internal
guidance system therefore when we give ourselves permission to express ourselves
we are choosing to honour and accept all parts of us and that includes our so-
called shadow self.*

DAILY MANTRA

"You are the subject in your life and all lessons assist you to develop key disciplines. Just know that all things are connected"
Rev Dr Trevor Adams

#23 YOU ABSOLUTELY CAN HAVE IT ALL

When I came to realise that I absolutely can have it all! that was the
difference that made the difference.
Mindset-Reset Now!

RESPONSIBILITY

*When you come to realise that you absolutely can have it all! that will be the
difference that will make the difference.* It is your responsibility to tune your
mindset to abundance in all areas of your life. *You can either watch the
movie, be in the movie, direct the movie or you can produce the movie.*

MANAGEMENT

*When you come to realise that you absolutely can have it all! that will be the
difference that will make the difference.* Managing your mindset in
alignment with this realisation can shift your reality beyond belief. *In
life you are not defined by the things that happen to you, what matters most is
how you choose to respond to the contrast that shows up in your life and that
starts with having a fertile mindset.*

EXPRESSION

*When you come to realise that you absolutely can have it all! that will be the
difference that will make the difference.* This insight can lead you to a deep
sense of self-expression beyond your wildest dream. *I believe that our
emotions are merely our internal guidance system therefore when we give ourselves
permission to express ourselves we are choosing to honour and accept all parts of
us and that includes our so-called shadow self.*

DAILY MANTRA

"You absolutely can have it all!" Regan Hillyer

#24 YOUR CORE

When I grew to realise that connecting with my core is vital for my
longevity, I really began to awaken my giant within.
Mindset-Reset Now!

RESPONSIBILITY

*When you grow to realise that connecting with your core is vital for your longevity,
you will really begin to awaken your giant within.* It's your responsibility to
connect to your core self opens you up to a world of possibilities
beyond your wildest dreams. You'll connect to your original story,
your primary emotions, your dreams and your deepest desires. *You
can either watch the movie, be in the movie, direct the movie or you can produce
the movie.*

MANAGEMENT

*When you grow to realise that connecting with your core is vital for your longevity,
you will really begin to awaken your giant within.* Learning to manage and
maintain your connecting with your inner core is a good starting
place. *In life you are not defined by the things that happen to you, what matters
most is how you choose to respond to the contrast that shows up in your life and
that starts with having a fertile mindset.*

EXPRESSION

*When you shift your mindset to self-belief, surrender to the process and trust your
intuition that will be the difference that will make the difference.* Establishing
a deep sense of connection with your inner core will empower you
to express yourself from an entirely new level. *I believe that our emotions
are merely our internal guidance system therefore when we give ourselves
permission to express ourselves we are choosing to honour and accept all parts of
us and that includes our so-called shadow self.*

DAILY MANTRA

"Connect to your core." Juan Pablo Barahona

#25 YOUTH EVOLUTION – BOOM!

When I learned how to take a good look at myself and my
surrounding world of youth that are co-creating a Youth
Revolution – BOOM! Now that was the difference that makes the
difference.
Mindset-Reset Now!

RESPONSIBILITY

*When you learn how to take a good look at yourself and your surrounding world
of youth that are co-creating a Youth Revolution – BOOM! Now that's the
difference that'll make the difference.* I am really passionate about
reminding children and youth and also the inner child in adults to
come out and play. I enjoy asking adults to take responsibility to
support the development of the youth of today as they'll become the
leaders of tomorrow. *You can either watch the movie, be in the movie, direct
the movie or you can produce the movie.*

MANAGEMENT

*When you learn how to take a good look at yourself and your surrounding world
of youth that are co-creating a Youth Revolution – BOOM! Now that's the
difference that'll make the difference.* You have the ability to manage so
much more than you could imagine. *In life you are not defined by the
things that happen to you, what matters most is how you choose to respond to the
contrast that shows up in your life and that starts with having a fertile mindset.*

EXPRESSION

*When you learn how to take a good look at yourself and your surrounding world
of youth that are co-creating a Youth Revolution – BOOM! Now that's the
difference that'll make the difference.* I encourage you to plant your seed
in this playground that we get to call life. In order to do this, we first
must listen to the hearts and minds of the youth of today. *I believe
that our emotions are merely our internal guidance system therefore when we give
ourselves permission to express ourselves we are choosing to honour and accept all
parts of us and that includes our so-called shadow self.*

DAILY MANTRA

"Youth Revolution – BOOM!" 15yr old Daniel Barahona

#26 HEAL

When I learned about the connection between forgiveness and healing, that gave me a deep sense of peace.
Mindset-Reset Now!

RESPONSIBILITY

When I learned about the connection between forgiveness and healing, that gave me a deep sense of peace. I truly believe that the connection between forgiveness and healing is so deeply profound so take responsibility to allow yourself to let go and forgive so you can fully heal from your past. *You can either watch the movie, be in the movie, direct the movie or you can produce the movie.*

MANAGEMENT

When I learned about the connection between forgiveness and healing, that gave me a deep sense of peace. It is vital for you to manage your emotion so you can begin to heal your internal and external world. *In life you are not defined by the things that happen to you, what matters most is how you choose to respond to the contrast that shows up in your life and that starts with having a fertile mindset.*

EXPRESSION

When I learned about the connection between forgiveness and healing, that gave me a deep sense of peace. When you allow yourself to forgive and let go, you will be able to fully express yourself. *I believe that our emotions are merely our internal guidance system therefore when we give ourselves permission to express ourselves we are choosing to honour and accept all parts of us and that includes our so-called shadow self.*

DAILY MANTRA

"It's time to heal." Karen St Cyr

#27 WISDOM IS AGELESS

When I learned that wisdom is contained within the hearts and minds of all ages and that I could learn from them all, life really began to be fun.
Mindset-Reset Now!

RESPONSIBILITY

When you learn that wisdom is contained within the hearts and minds of all ages and that you can learn from them all, life can really begin to be fun. Take responsibility to receive wisdom from all ages. *You can either watch the movie, be in the movie, direct the movie or you can produce the movie.*

MANAGEMENT

When you learn that wisdom is contained within the hearts and minds of all ages and that you can learn from them all, life can really begin to be fun. Learn to manage your mindset to empower you to receive wisdom everywhere you go. *In life you are not defined by the things that happen to you, what matters most is how you choose to respond to the contrast that shows up in your life and that starts with having a fertile mindset.*

EXPRESSION

When you learn that wisdom is contained within the hearts and minds of all ages and that you can learn from them all, life can really begin to be fun. Allow the wisdom of others to empower your ability to express. *I believe that our emotions are merely our internal guidance system therefore when we give ourselves permission to express ourselves we are choosing to honour and accept all parts of us and that includes our so-called shadow self.*

DAILY MANTRA

"Wisdom is contained within the hearts and minds of all ages and I learn from them all." Dr Valentine

#28 SOULJAH KINGDOM RISE

When I close my eyes and imagine SoulJah Kingdom Rise, I get
really excited and visualise the infinite possibilities as a story
enriched with culture begins to take the world by storm.
Mindset-Reset Now!

RESPONSIBILITY

*When you close your eyes and imagine SoulJah Kingdom Rise, you can begin to
get really excited and visualise the infinite possibilities as a story enriched with
culture begins to take the world by storm.* SoulJah Kingdom Rise is calling
on you to take responsibility to go on a journey of cultural self-
discovery as a family. *You can either watch the movie, be in the movie, direct
the movie or you can produce the movie.*

MANAGEMENT

*When you close your eyes and imagine SoulJah Kingdom Rise, you can begin to
get really excited and visualise the infinite possibilities as a story enriched with
culture begins to take the world by storm.* Immersing yourself and your
family into this new reality will empower you to manage your family
dynamics in a phenomenal new way enriched with culture, adventure
and courage beyond your wildest dreams. *In life you are not defined by
the things that happen to you, what matters most is how you choose to respond to
the contrast that shows up in your life and that starts with having a fertile
mindset.*

EXPRESSION

*When you close your eyes and imagine SoulJah Kingdom Rise, you can begin to
get really excited and visualise the infinite possibilities as a story enriched with
culture begins to take the world by storm.* Once you immerse yourself into
this extraordinary new world, you will find a new sense of self
expression that is enriched with culture, wisdom and so much more.
*I believe that our emotions are merely our internal guidance system therefore when
we give ourselves permission to express ourselves we are choosing to honour and
accept all parts of us and that includes our so-called shadow self.*

DAILY MANTRA

"Close your eyes and imagine SoulJah Kingdom Rise." Winston Hislop

#29 GOD FIRST

When I learned to put God first, trusting that all things will follow,
my life began to shift in a truly remarkable way.
Mindset-Reset Now!

RESPONSIBILITY

When you learn to put God first, trusting that all things will follow, your life will begin to shift in a truly remarkable way. It is your responsibility to exercise your free will, however it is also important to know when to surrender to your spiritual journey. *You can either watch the movie, be in the movie, direct the movie or you can produce the movie.*

MANAGEMENT

When you learn to put God first, trusting that all things will follow, your life will begin to shift in a truly remarkable way. Learning to better manage your life starts with you being able to trust the process and adhere to divine guidance. *In life you are not defined by the things that happen to you, what matters most is how you choose to respond to the contrast that shows up in your life and that starts with having a fertile mindset.*

EXPRESSION

When you learn to put God first, trusting that all things will follow, your life will begin to shift in a truly remarkable way. When you put God first, your ability to express yourself can organically expand. *I believe that our emotions are merely our internal guidance system therefore when we give ourselves permission to express ourselves we are choosing to honour and accept all parts of us and that includes our so-called shadow self.*

DAILY MANTRA

"Put God first and all things will follow" Zabdiel Campbell

#30 GOD-INCIDENCE

When I chose to embrace God-incidence working in my life, my
heart filled with gratitude.
Mindset-Reset Now!

RESPONSIBILITY

*When you chose to embrace God-incidence working in your life, your heart will
fill with gratitude.* I truly believe that in life it is your responsibility to
maintain a positive, caring and kind character and allow God-
incidences to bring the right people, experiences and things into your
life. *You can either watch the movie, be in the movie, direct the movie or you can
produce the movie.*

MANAGEMENT

*When you chose to embrace God-incidence working in your life, your heart will
fill with gratitude.* Manage your character and watch the God-times
flow. *In life you are not defined by the things that happen to you, what matters
most is how you choose to respond to the contrast that shows up in your life and
that starts with having a fertile mindset.*

EXPRESSION

*When you chose to embrace God-incidence working in your life, your heart will
fill with gratitude.* Allow yourself to express your emotions freely so
you can become one with the essence of life. *I believe that our emotions
are merely our internal guidance system therefore when we give ourselves
permission to express ourselves we are choosing to honour and accept all parts of
us and that includes our so-called shadow self.*

DAILY MANTRA

"God-incidence." Rasheda Ashanti Malcolm

#31 GRATITUDE

When I learned that gratitude was the best starting point to allow things to flow into my life, this was the difference that made the difference.
Mindset-Reset Now!

RESPONSIBILITY

When you learn that gratitude is the best starting point to allow things to flow into your life, this will be the difference that makes the difference. Taking responsibility for the primary foundation that you seed into your life, that will be a game changer. *You can either watch the movie, be in the movie, direct the movie or you can produce the movie.*

MANAGEMENT

When you learn that gratitude is the best starting point to allow things to flow into your life, this will be the difference that makes the difference. Managing your life from a place of gratitude is a good idea. *In life you are not defined by the things that happen to you, what matters most is how you choose to respond to the contrast that shows up in your life and that starts with having a fertile mindset.*

EXPRESSION

When you learn that gratitude is the best starting point to allow things to flow into your life, this will be the difference that makes the difference. Sit back and watch your life transform when you choose to express yourself from a place of gratitude. *I believe that our emotions are merely our internal guidance system therefore when we give ourselves permission to express ourselves we are choosing to honour and accept all parts of us and that includes our so-called shadow self.*

DAILY MANTRA

"Gratitude." Rasher B McNeish

#32 EXPERIENTIAL

When I immersed myself into experiential learning, it totally transformed my learning experience.
Mindset-Reset Now!

RESPONSIBILITY

When you immerse yourself into experiential learning, it will totally transform your learning experience. Take responsibility to grant yourself permission to immerse yourself into new experiential experiences that will transform your reality forever. *You can either watch the movie, be in the movie, direct the movie or you can produce the movie.*

MANAGEMENT

When you immerse yourself into experiential learning, it will totally transform your learning experience. When you immerse yourself into experiential growth you will learn to manage yourself in an entirely new way. *In life you are not defined by the things that happen to you, what matters most is how you choose to respond to the contrast that shows up in your life and that starts with having a fertile mindset.*

EXPRESSION

When you immerse yourself into experiential learning, it will totally transform your learning experience. Your ability to express yourself will take on an entirely new meaning. *I believe that our emotions are merely our internal guidance system therefore when we give ourselves permission to express ourselves we are choosing to honour and accept all parts of us and that includes our so-called shadow self.*

DAILY MANTRA

"Experiential learning is the difference that will make the difference." Sabrina Ben Salmi BSc aka Dura Mater

#33 LAY THE FOUNDATION

When I grew to realise that Pray is the foundation from which all things are possible, that was the difference that made the difference.
Mindset-Reset Now!

RESPONSIBILITY

When you grow to realise that Pray is the foundation from which all things become possible, that will be the difference that will make the difference. Take the responsibility to become a King/Queen/Prince/Princess in the Kingdom of pray, then take a step back to observe all areas of your life improve (including your relationships) in the most profound ways. *You can either watch the movie, be in the movie, direct the movie or you can produce the movie.*

MANAGEMENT

When you grow to realise that Pray is the foundation from which all things become possible, that will be the difference that will make the difference. Learn to manage your state, maintain faith, surrender to pray and trust the process. *In life you are not defined by the things that happen to you, what matters most is how you choose to respond to the contrast that shows up in your life and that starts with having a fertile mindset.*

EXPRESSION

When you grow to realise that Pray is the foundation from which all things become possible, that will be the difference that will make the difference. Deepening your ability to express yourself in any given situation will empower you to connect with unexpected pleasantries in abundance. *I believe that our emotions are merely our internal guidance system therefore when we give ourselves permission to express ourselves we are choosing to honour and accept all parts of us and that includes our so-called shadow self.*

DAILY MANTRA

"Pray is the foundation from which all things are possible."
Priscilla Madu aka Pray Queen

#34 PEER TO PEER

When I learned about the importance of peer to peer learning, I
got stuck in, so I could enjoy the experience.
Mindset-Reset Now!

RESPONSIBILITY

When you learn about the importance of peer to peer learning, get stuck in and enjoy the experience. It is proven that peer to peer learning have a positive impact on your confidence and independence in learning and you gain a deeper understanding. It is your responsibility to be the best that you can be. *You can either watch the movie, be in the movie, direct the movie or you can produce the movie.*

MANAGEMENT

When you learn about the importance of peer to peer learning, get stuck in and enjoy the experience. Peer to peer learning can help you to improve the way you manage your life. *In life you are not defined by the things that happen to you, what matters most is how you choose to respond to the contrast that shows up in your life and that starts with having a fertile mindset.*

EXPRESSION

When you learn about the importance of peer to peer learning, get stuck in and enjoy the experience. Peer to peer learning is the difference that will make the difference to the way you choose to express yourself. *I believe that our emotions are merely our internal guidance system therefore when we give ourselves permission to express ourselves we are choosing to honour and accept all parts of us and that includes our so-called shadow self.*

DAILY MANTRA

"Peer to peer learning is the difference that makes the difference."
Lesley Warren

#35 YOU BECOME WHAT YOU AFFIRM

When I became aware that I become what I affirm, I became more conscious about what I was choosing to affirm.
Mindset-Reset Now!

RESPONSIBILITY

When you become aware of the fact that you become what you affirm, you will become more conscious about what you are choosing to affirm. Take responsibility of what you affirm to yourself and others. *You can either watch the movie, be in the movie, direct the movie or you can produce the movie.*

MANAGEMENT

When you become aware of the fact that you become what you affirm, you will become more conscious about what you are choosing to affirm. Learn how to better manage your words so you can affirm more positivity into your life. *In life you are not defined by the things that happen to you, what matters most is how you choose to respond to the contrast that shows up in your life and that starts with having a fertile mindset.*

EXPRESSION

When you become aware of the fact that you become what you affirm, you will become more conscious about what you are choosing to affirm. Expressing yourself through positive affirmation will transform your mind. *I believe that our emotions are merely our internal guidance system therefore when we give ourselves permission to express ourselves we are choosing to honour and accept all parts of us and that includes our so-called shadow self.*

DAILY MANTRA

"You become what you affirm." 7yr old Amire Ben Salmi aka Mr Intelligent

#36 THE CHOICE IS YOURS

When I came to realise the fact that the choice is mine, things
began to make sense.
Mindset-Reset Now!

RESPONSIBILITY

*When you come to realise the fact that the choice is yours, things will begin to
make sense.* Take responsibility to consciously make choices in your
life. *You can either watch the movie, be in the movie, direct the movie or you can
produce the movie.*

MANAGEMENT

*When you shift your mindset to self-belief, surrender to the process and trust your
intuition that will be the difference that will make the difference.* Managing the
choices that you have in your life is key. *In life you are not defined by the
things that happen to you, what matters most is how you choose to respond to the
contrast that shows up in your life and that starts with having a fertile mindset.*

EXPRESSION

*When you shift your mindset to self-belief, surrender to the process and trust your
intuition that will be the difference that will make the difference.* Empower
yourself by giving yourself permission to express your authentic self
as often as possible. *I believe that our emotions are merely our internal
guidance system therefore when we give ourselves permission to express ourselves
we are choosing to honour and accept all parts of us and that includes our so-
called shadow self.*

DAILY MANTRA

"Always remember that the choice is yours." 13yr old Yasmine Ben
Salmi aka Loveprenure

#37 CHANGE

When I came to realise the fact that in a split second my life can change, and that it was up to me how I choose to respond to that which presents, I began to soar.
Mindset-Reset Now!

RESPONSIBILITY

When you realise that in a split second your life can change, and that it is up to you how you choose to respond to that which presents, you will begin to soar. It is your responsibility to respond in the best possible way. *You can either watch the movie, be in the movie, direct the movie or you can produce the movie.*

MANAGEMENT

When you realise that in a split second your life can change, and that it is up to you how you choose to respond to that which presents, you will begin to soar. I believe in you and I know that you will do what it takes to best manage your life. *In life you are not defined by the things that happen to you, what matters most is how you choose to respond to the contrast that shows up in your life and that starts with having a fertile mindset.*

EXPRESSION

When you realise that in a split second your life can change, and that it is up to you how you choose to respond to that which presents, you will begin to soar. Express yourself from a place of authenticity. *I believe that our emotions are merely our internal guidance system therefore when we give ourselves permission to express ourselves we are choosing to honour and accept all parts of us and that includes our so-called shadow self.*

DAILY MANTRA

"In a split second your life can change, it is up to you how you choose respond." 16yr old Tray-Sean Ben Salmi aka T7 (T = Tray-Sean/Testimony/Truth + 7 = Complete)

#38 NO ONE CAN DANCE YOUR DANCE

When I grew to realise the fact that no one can walk my walk, no one can sing my song, and no one can dance my dance; because I am unique, perfect and beautiful just the way I am – so I will not allow my dreams to die inside of me.
Mindset-Reset Now!

RESPONSIBILITY

When you grow to realise the fact that no one can walk your walk, no one can sing your song, and no one can dance your dance – because you are unique, perfect and beautiful just the way you are. Promise yourself that you will not allow your dreams to die inside of you. take responsibility to honour your inner calling and share your message with the world. *You can either watch the movie, be in the movie, direct the movie or you can produce the movie.*

MANAGEMENT

When you grow to realise the fact that no one can walk your walk, no one can sing your song, and no one can dance your dance – because you are unique, perfect and beautiful just the way you are. Promise yourself that you will not allow your dreams to die inside of you. managing your world from a place of passion and purpose can yield you huge results. *In life you are not defined by the things that happen to you, what matters most is how you choose to respond to the contrast that shows up in your life and that starts with having a fertile mindset.*

EXPRESSION

When you grow to realise the fact that no one can walk your walk, no one can sing your song, and no one can dance your dance – because you are unique, perfect and beautiful just the way you are. Promise yourself that you will not allow your dreams to die inside of you. Grant yourself permission to fully express you inner calling with the world. *I believe that our emotions are merely our internal guidance system therefore when we give ourselves permission to express ourselves we are choosing to honour and accept all parts of us and that includes our so-called shadow self.*

DAILY MANTRA

"No one can walk your walk, no one can sing your song, and no one can dance your dance. You are unique, perfect and beautiful just the way you are – so do not allow your dreams to die inside of you." 20yr old Lashai Ben Salmi

#39 THE JOURNEY

When I came to realise that we are only passing through this life,
and that it's wise to choose to do so with love and care. This gave
me an entirely new perspective of life.
Mindset-Reset Now!

RESPONSIBILITY

When you come to realise that we are only passing through this life, and that it's wise to choose to do so with love and care. This will give you an entirely new perspective of life. I believe that you should take full responsibility in your life instead of giving your power away by running around aimlessly in life like sheeple. It is time to STEP into your POWER which is your divine birth right sovereignty to action your freewill and create your desired lifestyle. *You can either watch the movie, be in the movie, direct the movie or you can produce the movie.*

MANAGEMENT

When you come to realise that we are only passing through this life, and that it's wise to choose to do so with love and care. This will give you an entirely new perspective of life. Learning to manage the way that you treat yourself and others will create a sense of peace in your life. *In life you are not defined by the things that happen to you, what matters most is how you choose to respond to the contrast that shows up in your life and that starts with having a fertile mindset.*

EXPRESSION

When you come to realise that we are only passing through this life, and that it's wise to choose to do so with love and care. This will give you an entirely new perspective of life. Expression is vital for your inner peace. *I believe that our emotions are merely our internal guidance system therefore when we give ourselves permission to express ourselves we are choosing to honour and accept all parts of us and that includes our so-called shadow self.*

DAILY MANTRA

"We are only passing through this life, therefore choose do so with love and care." Mary Paul aka Nan

#40 SMILE

When I learned about the BENEFITS of LAUGHTER &
SMILING, it took my energy to a whole new level of inner peace.
Mindset-Reset Now!

RESPONSIBILITY

*When you learn about the BENEFITS of LAUGHTER & SMILING,
it will take your energy to a whole new level of inner peace.* I encourage you
to take responsibility for your happiness. *You can either watch the movie,
be in the movie, direct the movie or you can produce the movie.*

MANAGEMENT

*When you learn about the BENEFITS of LAUGHTER & SMILING,
it will take your energy to a whole new level of inner peace.* Make managing
your inner peace your priority. *In life you are not defined by the things that
happen to you, what matters most is how you choose to respond to the contrast
that shows up in your life and that starts with having a fertile mindset.*

EXPRESSION

*When you learn about the BENEFITS of LAUGHTER & SMILING,
it will take your energy to a whole new level of inner peace.* Express yourself
in ways that make you laugh and smile both inside and out. *I believe
that our emotions are merely our internal guidance system therefore when we give
ourselves permission to express ourselves we are choosing to honour and accept all
parts of us and that includes our so-called shadow self.*

DAILY MANTRA

"LAUGH & SMILE." Honourable Kizito - Nollywood

#43 THE JOURNEY

When I came to realise the infinite possibilities of rebuilding Africa, I became inspired to create generational wealth that will go on to impact nations for generations to come.
Mindset-Reset Now!

RESPONSIBILITY

When you come to realise the infinite possibilities of rebuilding Africa, you will become inspired to create generational wealth that will go on to impact nations for generations to come. Take responsibility to show up in the world as your unique piece to the puzzle, and that alone will go on to generate huge ripple effects of possibilities. *You can either watch the movie, be in the movie, direct the movie or you can produce the movie.*

MANAGEMENT

When you come to realise the infinite possibilities of rebuilding Africa, you will become inspired to create generational wealth that will go on to impact nations for generations to come. Manage your state of being and all will be well. *In life you are not defined by the things that happen to you, what matters most is how you choose to respond to the contrast that shows up in your life and that starts with having a fertile mindset.*

EXPRESSION

When you come to realise the infinite possibilities of rebuilding Africa, you will become inspired to create generational wealth that will go on to impact nations for generations to come. Just know that your authentic expression is the secret to the success. *I believe that our emotions are merely our internal guidance system therefore when we give ourselves permission to express ourselves we are choosing to honour and accept all parts of us and that includes our so-called shadow self.*

DAILY MANTRA

"Do you know what we could do by rebuilding Africa?" HE Amb Arikana Chihombori Quao

#44 YOUR HEALTH IS YOUR WEALTH

When I came to the realisation that there is nothing on this earth
more precious than my health, wealth and happiness. I began to
deeply appreciate my health, wealth and happiness from a place of
deep gratitude.
Mindset-Reset Now!

RESPONSIBILITY

*When you come to the realisation that there is nothing on this earth more precious
than your health, wealth and happiness. You will begin to deeply appreciate the
health, wealth and happiness that you have in abundance from a place of deep
gratitude.* Now I want you to place your hands on your heart and then
take three deep breaths and say, "I am choosing to take responsibility
for my health, wealth and happiness right here and right now". Close
your eyes and allow yourself to just imagine your dreams becoming
a reality. *You can either watch the movie, be in the movie, direct the movie or
you can produce the movie.*

MANAGEMENT

*When you come to the realisation that there is nothing on this earth more precious
than your health, wealth and happiness. You will begin to deeply appreciate the
health, wealth and happiness that you have in abundance from a place of deep
gratitude.* Manage your emotion and trust that everything else will fall
into place. *In life you are not defined by the things that happen to you, what
matters most is how you choose to respond to the contrast that shows up in your
life and that starts with having a fertile mindset.*

EXPRESSION

*When you come to the realisation that there is nothing on this earth more precious
than your health, wealth and happiness. You will begin to deeply appreciate the
health, wealth and happiness that you have in abundance from a place of deep
gratitude.* Just know that it is safe to fully express yourself no matter
how you are feeling, just know that it is safe and okay to express
yourself now. *I believe that our emotions are merely our internal guidance
system therefore when we give ourselves permission to express ourselves we are*

choosing to honour and accept all parts of us and that includes our so-called shadow self.

DAILY MANTRA
"Your abundance shows up as your health, wealth and happiness."
Paolo Ben Salmi

#45 TREES

I grew in wisdom after hearing this scripture "Jeremiah 17:8 ESV /
341 helpful votes He is like a tree planted by water, that sends out
its roots by the stream, and does not fear when heat comes, for its
leaves remain green, and is not anxious in the year of drought, for
it does not cease to bear fruit". That was the difference that made
the difference.
Mindset-Reset Now!

RESPONSIBILITY

*You can grow in wisdom after hearing this scripture "Jeremiah 17:8 ESV /
341 helpful votes He is like a tree planted by water, that sends out its roots by
the stream, and does not fear when heat comes, for its leaves remain green, and is
not anxious in the year of drought, for it does not cease to bear fruit". This
scripture can have a huge impact on your mind, body and soul.* Take the
responsibility to take heed of wisdom when it is presented to you as
it has the power to transform the trajectory of your life. *You can either
watch the movie, be in the movie, direct the movie or you can produce the movie.*

MANAGEMENT

*You can grow in wisdom after hearing this scripture "Jeremiah 17:8 ESV /
341 helpful votes He is like a tree planted by water, that sends out its roots by
the stream, and does not fear when heat comes, for its leaves remain green, and is
not anxious in the year of drought, for it does not cease to bear fruit". This
scripture can have a huge impact on your mind, body and soul. Learn to* manage
the way you show up in life from this day forth. *In life you are not
defined by the things that happen to you, what matters most is how you choose to
respond to the contrast that shows up in your life and that starts with having a
fertile mindset.*

EXPRESSION

*You can grow in wisdom after hearing this scripture "Jeremiah 17:8 ESV /
341 helpful votes He is like a tree planted by water, that sends out its roots by
the stream, and does not fear when heat comes, for its leaves remain green, and is
not anxious in the year of drought, for it does not cease to bear fruit". This*

scripture can have a huge impact on your mind, body and soul. Wisdom empowers you to deepen your ability to express yourself. *I believe that our emotions are merely our internal guidance system therefore when we give ourselves permission to express ourselves we are choosing to honour and accept all parts of us and that includes our so-called shadow self.*

DAILY MANTRA

"Jeremiah 17:8 ESV / 341 helpful votes

He is like a tree planted by water, that sends out its roots by the stream, and does not fear when heat comes, for its leaves remain green, and is not anxious in the year of drought, for it does not cease to bear fruit." Apostle Linda Edwards

GIVE YOURSELF TIME
JOURNAL

GIVE YOURSELF TIME DAILY JOURNAL

Writing things down is an effective way of remembering and reflecting on all the amazing things that happen every day and it can transform your mindset.

No matter how much you write or how little you write take the time to really think about your day, at the end of your journal you can then go back and treasure those memories.

Date: __/__/____ Today I am Grateful For…

_____

_____

What Would Make Today A Great Day?

_____

_____

During the evening just before going to bed take a moment to reflect on your day then List the 3 best things that happened…

_____

_____

1) _____

2) _____

3) _____

Date: __/__/____ Today I am Grateful For…

_____

_____

What Would Make Today A Great Day?

_____

_____

During the evening just before going to bed take a moment to reflect on your day then List the 3 best things that happened...

1) _____

2) _____

3) _____

Date: __/__/____ Today I am Grateful For...

_____

_____

What Would Make Today A Great Day?

_____

_____

During the evening just before going to bed take a moment to reflect on your day then List the 3 best things that happened...

1) _____

2) _____

3) _____

Date: __/__/____ Today I am Grateful For...

_____

_____

What Would Make Today A Great Day?

_____

_____

During the evening just before going to bed take a moment to reflect on your day then List the 3 best things that happened...

1) _____

_____

2) _____

3) _____

Date: __/__/____ Today I am Grateful For...

_____

What Would Make Today A Great Day?

_____

During the evening just before going to bed take a moment to reflect on your day then List the 3 best things that happened...

1) _____

2) _____

3) _____

Date: __/__/____ Today I am Grateful For...

_____

What Would Make Today A Great Day?

_____

During the evening just before going to bed take a moment to reflect on your day then List the 3 best things that happened...

1) _____

2) _____

3) _____
   _____

Date: __/__/____ Today I am Grateful For...

_____
_____

What Would Make Today A Great Day?

_____
_____

During the evening just before going to bed take a moment to reflect on your day then List the 3 best things that happened...
1) _____
   _____
2) _____
   _____
3) _____
   _____

Date: __/__/____ Today I am Grateful For...

_____
_____

What Would Make Today A Great Day?

_____
_____

During the evening just before going to bed take a moment to reflect on your day then List the 3 best things that happened...
1) _____
   _____
2) _____
   _____
3) _____
   _____

Date: __/__/____ Today I am Grateful For...

_____

_____

What Would Make Today A Great Day?

_____

_____

During the evening just before going to bed take a moment to reflect on your day then List the 3 best things that happened...

1) _____

_____

2) _____

_____

3) _____

_____

Date: __/__/____ Today I am Grateful For...

_____

_____

What Would Make Today A Great Day?

_____

_____

During the evening just before going to bed take a moment to reflect on your day then List the 3 best things that happened...

1) _____

_____

2) _____

_____

3) _____

_____

Date: __/__/____ Today I am Grateful For...

_____

_____

What Would Make Today A Great Day?

_____

_____

During the evening just before going to bed take a moment to reflect on your day then List the 3 best things that happened...

1) _____

_____

2) _____

_____

3) _____

_____

Date: __/__/____ Today I am Grateful For...

_____

_____

What Would Make Today A Great Day?

_____

_____

During the evening just before going to bed take a moment to reflect on your day then List the 3 best things that happened...

1) _____

_____

2) _____

_____

3) _____

_____

Date: __/__/____ Today I am Grateful For...

_____

_____

What Would Make Today A Great Day?

_____

_____

73

During the evening just before going to bed take a moment to reflect on your day then List the 3 best things that happened...

1) _____

2) _____

3) _____

Date: __/__/____ Today I am Grateful For...

What Would Make Today A Great Day?

During the evening just before going to bed take a moment to reflect on your day then List the 3 best things that happened...

1) _____

2) _____

3) _____

Date: __/__/____ Today I am Grateful For...

What Would Make Today A Great Day?

During the evening just before going to bed take a moment to reflect on your day then List the 3 best things that happened...

1) _____

2) _____

3) _____
_____

Date: __/__/____ Today I am Grateful For...

_____
_____

What Would Make Today A Great Day?

_____
_____

During the evening just before going to bed take a moment to reflect on your day then List the 3 best things that happened...

1) _____

2) _____

3) _____
_____

Date: __/__/____ Today I am Grateful For...

_____
_____

What Would Make Today A Great Day?

_____
_____

During the evening just before going to bed take a moment to reflect on your day then List the 3 best things that happened...

1) _____

2) _____
_____

3) _____
   _____

Date: __/__/____ Today I am Grateful For…

_____
_____

What Would Make Today A Great Day?

_____
_____

During the evening just before going to bed take a moment to reflect on your day then List the 3 best things that happened…
1) _____
2) _____
3) _____

Date: __/__/____ Today I am Grateful For…

_____
_____

What Would Make Today A Great Day?

_____
_____

During the evening just before going to bed take a moment to reflect on your day then List the 3 best things that happened…
1) _____
2) _____
3) _____

Date: __/__/____ Today I am Grateful For...

_____

_____

What Would Make Today A Great Day?

_____

_____

During the evening just before going to bed take a moment to reflect on your day then List the 3 best things that happened...

1) _____

_____

2) _____

_____

3) _____

_____

Date: __/__/____ Today I am Grateful For...

_____

_____

What Would Make Today A Great Day?

_____

_____

During the evening just before going to bed take a moment to reflect on your day then List the 3 best things that happened...

1) _____

_____

2) _____

_____

3) _____

_____

Date: __/__/____ Today I am Grateful For...

_____

_____

What Would Make Today A Great Day?

_____

_____

During the evening just before going to bed take a moment to
reflect on your day then List the 3 best things that happened...

1) _____

2) _____

3) _____

Date: __/__/____ Today I am Grateful For...

_____

_____

What Would Make Today A Great Day?

_____

_____

During the evening just before going to bed take a moment to
reflect on your day then List the 3 best things that happened...

1) _____

2) _____

3) _____

Date: __/__/____ Today I am Grateful For...

_____

_____

What Would Make Today A Great Day?

_____

_____

During the evening just before going to bed take a moment to reflect on your day then List the 3 best things that happened...
1) _____
_____
2) _____
_____
3) _____
_____

Date: __/__/____ Today I am Grateful For...

_____
_____

What Would Make Today A Great Day?

_____
_____

During the evening just before going to bed take a moment to reflect on your day then List the 3 best things that happened...
1) _____
_____
2) _____
_____
3) _____
_____

Date: __/__/____ Today I am Grateful For...

_____
_____

What Would Make Today A Great Day?

_____
_____

During the evening just before going to bed take a moment to reflect on your day then List the 3 best things that happened...
1) _____
_____

2) _____
_____

3) _____
_____

Date: __/__/____ Today I am Grateful For...

_____
_____

What Would Make Today A Great Day?

_____
_____

During the evening just before going to bed take a moment to reflect on your day then List the 3 best things that happened...

1) _____
_____

2) _____
_____

3) _____
_____

Date: __/__/____ Today I am Grateful For...

_____
_____

What Would Make Today A Great Day?

_____
_____

During the evening just before going to bed take a moment to reflect on your day then List the 3 best things that happened...

1) _____
_____

2) _____
_____

3) _____
_____

Date: __/__/____ Today I am Grateful For...

_____

_____

What Would Make Today A Great Day?

_____

_____

During the evening just before going to bed take a moment to reflect on your day then List the 3 best things that happened...

1) _____

2) _____

3) _____

Date: __/__/____ Today I am Grateful For...

_____

_____

What Would Make Today A Great Day?

_____

_____

During the evening just before going to bed take a moment to reflect on your day then List the 3 best things that happened...

1) _____

2) _____

3) _____

Date: __/__/____ Today I am Grateful For...

_____

What Would Make Today A Great Day?

During the evening just before going to bed take a moment to reflect on your day then List the 3 best things that happened...

1) _____

2) _____

3) _____

Date: ___/___/_____ Today I am Grateful For...

What Would Make Today A Great Day?

During the evening just before going to bed take a moment to reflect on your day then List the 3 best things that happened...

1) _____

2) _____

3) _____

Date: ___/___/_____ Today I am Grateful For...

What Would Make Today A Great Day?

During the evening just before going to bed take a moment to reflect on your day then List the 3 best things that happened…
1) _____
2) _____
3) _____

Date: __/__/____ Today I am Grateful For…

What Would Make Today A Great Day?

During the evening just before going to bed take a moment to reflect on your day then List the 3 best things that happened…
1) _____
2) _____
3) _____

Date: __/__/____ Today I am Grateful For…

What Would Make Today A Great Day?

During the evening just before going to bed take a moment to reflect on your day then List the 3 best things that happened…

1) _____

2) _____

3) _____

Date: __/__/____ Today I am Grateful For...

_____
_____

What Would Make Today A Great Day?

_____
_____

During the evening just before going to bed take a moment to reflect on your day then List the 3 best things that happened...

1) _____

2) _____

3) _____

Date: __/__/____ Today I am Grateful For...

_____
_____

What Would Make Today A Great Day?

_____
_____

During the evening just before going to bed take a moment to reflect on your day then List the 3 best things that happened...

1) _____

2) _____

3) _____

_____

Date: __/__/____ Today I am Grateful For...

_____

_____

What Would Make Today A Great Day?

_____

_____

During the evening just before going to bed take a moment to reflect on your day then List the 3 best things that happened...

1) _____

_____

2) _____

_____

3) _____

_____

Date: __/__/____ Today I am Grateful For...

_____

_____

What Would Make Today A Great Day?

_____

_____

During the evening just before going to bed take a moment to reflect on your day then List the 3 best things that happened...

1) _____

_____

2) _____

_____

3) _____

_____

Date: __/__/____ Today I am Grateful For...

_____

_____

What Would Make Today A Great Day?

_____

_____

During the evening just before going to bed take a moment to reflect on your day then List the 3 best things that happened...

1) _____

2) _____

3) _____

Date: __/__/____ Today I am Grateful For...

_____

_____

What Would Make Today A Great Day?

_____

_____

During the evening just before going to bed take a moment to reflect on your day then List the 3 best things that happened...

1) _____

2) _____

3) _____

Date: __/__/____ Today I am Grateful For...

_____

_____

What Would Make Today A Great Day?

During the evening just before going to bed take a moment to reflect on your day then List the 3 best things that happened...

1) _____

2) _____

3) _____

Date: __/__/____ Today I am Grateful For...

_____

_____

What Would Make Today A Great Day?

_____

_____

During the evening just before going to bed take a moment to reflect on your day then List the 3 best things that happened...

1) _____

2) _____

3) _____

Date: __/__/____ Today I am Grateful For...

_____

_____

What Would Make Today A Great Day?

_____

_____

During the evening just before going to bed take a moment to reflect on your day then List the 3 best things that happened...

1) _____

_____

2) _____

_____

3) _____

_____

Date: __/__/____ Today I am Grateful For...

_____

_____

What Would Make Today A Great Day?

_____

_____

During the evening just before going to bed take a moment to reflect on your day then List the 3 best things that happened...

1) _____

_____

2) _____

_____

3) _____

_____

Date: __/__/____ Today I am Grateful For...

_____

_____

What Would Make Today A Great Day?

_____

_____

During the evening just before going to bed take a moment to reflect on your day then List the 3 best things that happened...

1) _____

_____

2) _____

3) _____

Date: __/__/____ Today I am Grateful For...

_____

_____

What Would Make Today A Great Day?

_____

_____

During the evening just before going to bed take a moment to reflect on your day then List the 3 best things that happened...

1) _____

2) _____

3) _____

Date: __/__/____ Today I am Grateful For...

_____

_____

What Would Make Today A Great Day?

_____

_____

During the evening just before going to bed take a moment to reflect on your day then List the 3 best things that happened...

1) _____

2) _____

3) _____

Date: __/__/____ Today I am Grateful For…

_____

_____

What Would Make Today A Great Day?

_____

_____

During the evening just before going to bed take a moment to reflect on your day then List the 3 best things that happened…

1) _____

_____

2) _____

_____

3) _____

_____

Date: __/__/____ Today I am Grateful For…

_____

_____

What Would Make Today A Great Day?

_____

_____

During the evening just before going to bed take a moment to reflect on your day then List the 3 best things that happened…

1) _____

_____

2) _____

_____

3) _____

_____

Date: __/__/____ Today I am Grateful For…

_____

_____

What Would Make Today A Great Day?

_____

_____

During the evening just before going to bed take a moment to reflect on your day then List the 3 best things that happened...

1) _____

2) _____

3) _____

Date: __/__/____ Today I am Grateful For...

_____

_____

What Would Make Today A Great Day?

_____

_____

During the evening just before going to bed take a moment to reflect on your day then List the 3 best things that happened...

1) _____

2) _____

3) _____

Date: __/__/____ Today I am Grateful For...

_____

_____

What Would Make Today A Great Day?

_____

_____

During the evening just before going to bed take a moment to reflect on your day then List the 3 best things that happened...

1) _____

2) _____

3) _____

Date: __/__/____ Today I am Grateful For...

_____

_____

What Would Make Today A Great Day?

_____

_____

During the evening just before going to bed take a moment to reflect on your day then List the 3 best things that happened...

1) _____

2) _____

3) _____

Date: __/__/____ Today I am Grateful For...

_____

_____

What Would Make Today A Great Day?

_____

_____

During the evening just before going to bed take a moment to reflect on your day then List the 3 best things that happened...

1) _____

2) _____

3) _____

Date: __/__/____ Today I am Grateful For...

_____

_____

What Would Make Today A Great Day?

_____

_____

During the evening just before going to bed take a moment to reflect on your day then List the 3 best things that happened...

1) _____

2) _____

3) _____

Date: __/__/____ Today I am Grateful For...

_____

_____

What Would Make Today A Great Day?

_____

_____

During the evening just before going to bed take a moment to reflect on your day then List the 3 best things that happened...

1) _____

2) _____

3) _____
_____

Date: __/__/_____ Today I am Grateful For...

_____
_____

What Would Make Today A Great Day?

_____
_____

During the evening just before going to bed take a moment to reflect on your day then List the 3 best things that happened...

1) _____
_____

2) _____
_____

3) _____
_____

Date: __/__/_____ Today I am Grateful For...

_____
_____

What Would Make Today A Great Day?

_____
_____

During the evening just before going to bed take a moment to reflect on your day then List the 3 best things that happened...

1) _____
_____

2) _____
_____

3) _____
_____

Date: __/__/____ Today I am Grateful For...

_____

_____

What Would Make Today A Great Day?

_____

_____

During the evening just before going to bed take a moment to reflect on your day then List the 3 best things that happened...

1) _____

2) _____

3) _____

Date: __/__/____ Today I am Grateful For...

_____

_____

What Would Make Today A Great Day?

_____

_____

During the evening just before going to bed take a moment to reflect on your day then List the 3 best things that happened...

1) _____

2) _____

3) _____

Date: __/__/____ Today I am Grateful For...

_____

_____

What Would Make Today A Great Day?

_____

_____

During the evening just before going to bed take a moment to reflect on your day then List the 3 best things that happened...

1) _____

2) _____

3) _____

Date: __/__/____ Today I am Grateful For...

_____

_____

What Would Make Today A Great Day?

_____

_____

During the evening just before going to bed take a moment to reflect on your day then List the 3 best things that happened...

1) _____

2) _____

3) _____

Date: __/__/____ Today I am Grateful For...

_____

_____

What Would Make Today A Great Day?

_____

_____

During the evening just before going to bed take a moment to reflect on your day then List the 3 best things that happened...

1) _____

2) _____

3) _____

Date: __/__/____ Today I am Grateful For...

_____

_____

What Would Make Today A Great Day?

_____

_____

During the evening just before going to bed take a moment to reflect on your day then List the 3 best things that happened...

1) _____

2) _____

3) _____

Date: __/__/____ Today I am Grateful For...

_____

_____

What Would Make Today A Great Day?

_____

_____

During the evening just before going to bed take a moment to reflect on your day then List the 3 best things that happened...

1) _____

2) _____
_____

3) _____
_____

Date: __/__/____ Today I am Grateful For...

_____

_____

What Would Make Today A Great Day?

_____

_____

During the evening just before going to bed take a moment to reflect on your day then List the 3 best things that happened...

1) _____
_____

2) _____
_____

3) _____
_____

Date: __/__/____ Today I am Grateful For...

_____

_____

What Would Make Today A Great Day?

_____

_____

During the evening just before going to bed take a moment to reflect on your day then List the 3 best things that happened...

1) _____
_____

2) _____
_____

3) _____
_____

Date: __/__/____ Today I am Grateful For...

_____

_____

What Would Make Today A Great Day?

_____

_____

During the evening just before going to bed take a moment to reflect on your day then List the 3 best things that happened...

1) _____

_____

2) _____

_____

3) _____

_____

Date: __/__/____ Today I am Grateful For...

_____

_____

What Would Make Today A Great Day?

_____

_____

During the evening just before going to bed take a moment to reflect on your day then List the 3 best things that happened...

1) _____

_____

2) _____

_____

3) _____

_____

Date: __/__/____ Today I am Grateful For...

_____

What Would Make Today A Great Day?

During the evening just before going to bed take a moment to reflect on your day then List the 3 best things that happened...

1) _____

2) _____

3) _____

Date: __/__/____ Today I am Grateful For...

What Would Make Today A Great Day?

During the evening just before going to bed take a moment to reflect on your day then List the 3 best things that happened...

1) _____

2) _____

3) _____

Date: __/__/____ Today I am Grateful For...

What Would Make Today A Great Day?

During the evening just before going to bed take a moment to reflect on your day then List the 3 best things that happened...

1) _____

2) _____

3) _____

Date: __/__/____ Today I am Grateful For...

_____

_____

What Would Make Today A Great Day?

_____

_____

During the evening just before going to bed take a moment to reflect on your day then List the 3 best things that happened...

1) _____

2) _____

3) _____

Date: __/__/____ Today I am Grateful For...

_____

_____

What Would Make Today A Great Day?

_____

_____

During the evening just before going to bed take a moment to reflect on your day then List the 3 best things that happened...

1) _____

2) _____

3) _____

Date: __/__/____ Today I am Grateful For...

_____

_____

What Would Make Today A Great Day?

_____

_____

During the evening just before going to bed take a moment to reflect on your day then List the 3 best things that happened...

1) _____

2) _____

3) _____

Date: __/__/____ Today I am Grateful For...

_____

_____

What Would Make Today A Great Day?

_____

_____

During the evening just before going to bed take a moment to reflect on your day then List the 3 best things that happened...

1) _____

2) _____

3) _____
   _____

Date: __/__/____ Today I am Grateful For...

_____
_____

What Would Make Today A Great Day?

_____
_____

During the evening just before going to bed take a moment to reflect on your day then List the 3 best things that happened...

1) _____
   _____
2) _____
   _____
3) _____
   _____

Date: __/__/____ Today I am Grateful For...

_____
_____

What Would Make Today A Great Day?

_____
_____

During the evening just before going to bed take a moment to reflect on your day then List the 3 best things that happened...

1) _____
   _____
2) _____
   _____
3) _____
   _____

Date: __/__/____ Today I am Grateful For...

_____

_____

What Would Make Today A Great Day?

_____

_____

During the evening just before going to bed take a moment to
reflect on your day then List the 3 best things that happened...

1) _____

2) _____

3) _____

Date: __/__/____ Today I am Grateful For...

_____

_____

What Would Make Today A Great Day?

_____

_____

During the evening just before going to bed take a moment to
reflect on your day then List the 3 best things that happened...

1) _____

2) _____

3) _____

Date: __/__/____ Today I am Grateful For...

_____

_____

What Would Make Today A Great Day?

_____

_____

During the evening just before going to bed take a moment to
reflect on your day then List the 3 best things that happened...

1) _____

2) _____

3) _____

Date: __/__/____ Today I am Grateful For...

_____

_____

What Would Make Today A Great Day?

_____

_____

During the evening just before going to bed take a moment to
reflect on your day then List the 3 best things that happened...

1) _____

2) _____

3) _____

Date: __/__/____ Today I am Grateful For...

_____

_____

What Would Make Today A Great Day?

_____

_____

During the evening just before going to bed take a moment to reflect on your day then List the 3 best things that happened...

1) _____

2) _____

3) _____

Date: __/__/____ Today I am Grateful For...

_____

_____

What Would Make Today A Great Day?

_____

_____

During the evening just before going to bed take a moment to reflect on your day then List the 3 best things that happened...

1) _____

2) _____

3) _____

Date: __/__/____ Today I am Grateful For...

_____

_____

What Would Make Today A Great Day?

_____

_____

During the evening just before going to bed take a moment to reflect on your day then List the 3 best things that happened...

1) _____

_____

2) _____

3) _____

Date: __/__/____ Today I am Grateful For...

_____

_____

What Would Make Today A Great Day?

_____

_____

During the evening just before going to bed take a moment to reflect on your day then List the 3 best things that happened...

1) _____

2) _____

3) _____

Date: __/__/____ Today I am Grateful For...

_____

_____

What Would Make Today A Great Day?

_____

_____

During the evening just before going to bed take a moment to reflect on your day then List the 3 best things that happened...

1) _____

2) _____

3) _____

Date: __/__/____ Today I am Grateful For...

_____

_____

What Would Make Today A Great Day?

_____

_____

During the evening just before going to bed take a moment to reflect on your day then List the 3 best things that happened...

1) _____

2) _____

3) _____

Date: __/__/____ Today I am Grateful For...

_____

_____

What Would Make Today A Great Day?

_____

_____

During the evening just before going to bed take a moment to reflect on your day then List the 3 best things that happened...

1) _____

2) _____

3) _____

Date: __/__/____ Today I am Grateful For...

_____

What Would Make Today A Great Day?

During the evening just before going to bed take a moment to reflect on your day then List the 3 best things that happened...

1) _____

2) _____

3) _____

Date: __/__/____ Today I am Grateful For...

What Would Make Today A Great Day?

During the evening just before going to bed take a moment to reflect on your day then List the 3 best things that happened...

1) _____

2) _____

3) _____

Date: __/__/____ Today I am Grateful For...

What Would Make Today A Great Day?

During the evening just before going to bed take a moment to reflect on your day then List the 3 best things that happened...

1) _____

2) _____

3) _____

Date: __/__/____ Today I am Grateful For...

_____

_____

What Would Make Today A Great Day?

_____

_____

During the evening just before going to bed take a moment to reflect on your day then List the 3 best things that happened...

1) _____

2) _____

3) _____

Date: __/__/____ Today I am Grateful For...

_____

_____

What Would Make Today A Great Day?

_____

_____

During the evening just before going to bed take a moment to reflect on your day then List the 3 best things that happened...

1) _____

2) _____

3) _____

Date: __/__/____ Today I am Grateful For...

_____

_____

What Would Make Today A Great Day?

_____

_____

During the evening just before going to bed take a moment to
reflect on your day then List the 3 best things that happened...

1) _____

2) _____

3) _____

Date: __/__/____ Today I am Grateful For...

_____

_____

What Would Make Today A Great Day?

_____

_____

During the evening just before going to bed take a moment to
reflect on your day then List the 3 best things that happened...

1) _____

2) _____

3) _____

_____

Date: __/__/____ Today I am Grateful For...

_____

_____

What Would Make Today A Great Day?

_____

_____

During the evening just before going to bed take a moment to reflect on your day then List the 3 best things that happened...

1) _____

_____

2) _____

_____

3) _____

_____

Date: __/__/____ Today I am Grateful For...

_____

_____

What Would Make Today A Great Day?

_____

_____

During the evening just before going to bed take a moment to reflect on your day then List the 3 best things that happened...

1) _____

_____

2) _____

_____

3) _____

_____

PINT SIZE ADVENTURER - MINDSET IS KEY

Date: __/__/____ Today I am Grateful For...

_____

_____

What Would Make Today A Great Day?

_____

_____

During the evening just before going to bed take a moment to
reflect on your day then List the 3 best things that happened...

1) _____

2) _____

3) _____

A MESSAGE FROM ME TO YOU

I believe in you…

Be yourself no matter what and know that you are your biggest fan, always remember that life is a journey of market research and what you choose to do with it is up to you. take responsibility for your actions and word and surrender to the internal journey of self-discovery and the external journey out in this beautiful world that we get to call Earth.

Trust your highest thought, your clearest words and your grandest feeling? Your highest thought is always the thought which makes your feel good. Your clearest words are the words which contain truth and honesty. Your grandest feeling is LOVE
Paolo Ben Salmi

ABOUT THE AUTHOR

AS SEEN OF TV, RADIO & NEWSPAPERS

Paolo is also UK and African Ambassador to Global Diaspora United Voices for Economic Empowerment Forum

UK Ambassador of the Borg Banking Group AND of Borg University of International Skills.

Podcast Show Host of Life according To Paolo:
https://paolobensalmi.sounder.fm/show/life-according-to-paolo

Paolo is the youngest ever Water-to-Go Ambassador:
WWW.WATERTOGO.EU/PARTNERSHIPS/PAOLOB ENSALMI

Paolo and his family are the UK Associates for 360Wise Media
www.360wisemedia.com

Paolo is founded of SARVA

LinkedIn profile: http://linkedin.com/in/multiple-award-winning-author-paolo-ben-salmi-aka-p-573145194

11yr old Paolo Ben Salmi aka Pint Size Adventurer is not is not your average 11yr old.

Paolo was chosen to develop UnLtd application process together with his mother, big brother and big sister

Paolo works in partnership with Brunel University alongside his mother and four siblings aged 20, 15, 12 and 7 (who's the youngest ever STEM ambassador for Brunel University)

Paolo is the youngest ever member of the Wisdom
Council:
https://www.facebook.com/990806777731137/posts/212
8059590672511/?d=n

Paolo is proud to be a brand Ambassador for VueBox,
Choose Love and TruChallenge

My family and I have been acknowledged in the credits of a
NEW movie called: How Thoughts Become Things movie
promotional link:

Bit.ly/HowThoughtsBecomeThingsMovie2020

Paolo and his family held their signature 2 Day Family
workshop called Dreaming Big Together - Mamas Secret
Recipe at The Hub Chelsea FC

Water-to-Go blog about Paolo:
https://www.watertogo.eu/blog/meet-paolo-water-to-gos-
youngest-ever-ambassador/

Paolo is the founder of his own publishing house called
Adventurous Publishing.

Paolo hosted his signature program called Pint Size
Adventurer - The Abundant Adventure Creator™ at the
prestigious Virgin Money Lounge:
London Haymarket: Pint Size Adventurer - The Abundant
Adventure Creator - My Virgin Money

Paolo has interviewed people like Harry Hugo, Travis W
Fox, Douglas Vermeeren, Bernado Mayo, Bob Doyle,
Meagen Fettes, Udo Erasmus and Dr John Demartini to
name a few.

Paolo Ben Salmi is an award-winning author of the book
series called Pint Size Adventurer - 10 Keys Principles to Get
Your KIDS off their iPads & Into the Wild.

Paolo is an Award-Winning Public Speaker (who has spoken at eleventh such as Mercedes Benz World and Virgin etc.)

Paolo has participated in brand campaigns for Sainsburys, Legoland, Matr, Warner Bros, Sony and Made for Mums to name a few.

TruLittle Heros Award - U12 Entreprenur 2017, Guest speaker at The Beat You Expo: https://youtu.be/Fz9mErJC8rA where there were 15,000 attendees

Mercedes Benz World, Official Judge for Made for Mums Toy Awards 2018 via Team Trouble, Former International Radio Show host

Thanks to Douglas Vermeeren back in 2017 Paolo made history by being the youngest to interview Dr. John Demartini: https://www.facebook.com/350400542063654/videos/36 3072487463126/

Paolo has spoken on stage alongside people such as: Dr John Demartini, Douglas Vermeeren, Dr Toby Bailey, He Amb Arikana Chihombori Quao, Sir Dr Joe Madu, Sesh Sukhdeo, Prof. Chimezie, Dr Debbie Bartlett, Amb.(Rtd) Robert Perry, Robert Barnard-Weston, Col Brian Searcy (Rtd-USAF), Lamido Umar, Keston White-Marin, Evelyn Okpanachi, Prof. Abraham Osinubi, Alison Hall, Gunter Pauli, Steven Fern, Kanayo O. Kanayo and Hon. Kizito Ikenna to name a few.

Paolo is a personal developments coach and founder of Pint Size Adventurer who is here to help you to plant the seed toward self-discovery, exploration of the internal and external world and adventurer in abundance via a variety of products and services to assist you to create a brighter future

Paolo desires to encourage as many children as possible to go on adventures both internally and externally to activate their natural curiosity.

The question is are you watching the movie, in the movie or directing the movie?

Book:

Pint Sized Adventurer: The Abundant Adventure Creator
https://www.amazon.co.uk/PINT-SIZE-ADVENTURER-ABUNDANT-ADVENTURE/dp/1913310183/ref=tmm_pap_swatch_0?_encoding=UTF8&qid=1585959464&sr=1-1

Facebook page Pint Size Adventurer:
https://m.facebook.com/paolobensalmiakapintsizeadventurer/

BEN SALMI FAMILY MANTRA

"BEN SALMI TEAMWORK, MAKES THE
DREAMWORK

We believe that there is no such thing as failure only
feedback.

We also believe that the journey of one thousand miles
begins with a single step in the right direction

FAMILY ANTHEM

If you want to be somebody,
If you want to go somewhere,
You better wake up and PAY ATTENTION

I'm ready to be somebody,
I'm ready to go somewhere,
I'm ready to wake up and PAY ATTENTION!

The question is ARE YOU?

You're invited to GDE2
Zoom meeting ID: 84789704519 Passcode: 530431 to join
on Saturday Oct 24th 2020 @ Noon CST
image.png

Masters of: Branding, Human Capital Optimization &
Situational Awareness

image.png
https://www.youtube.com/watch?v=wuaYFxG6oFA&aut
huser=0

https://www.youtube.com/watch?v=fCrxL_0HDyA&auth
user=0

Grandmaster K.S.Lee

Grandmaster Kang Seok Lee

Grandmaster Kang Seok Lee grew up in a small village in
southern South Korea as the third of eight children. He
started his training in Tae Kwon Do when he was seven
years old because his parents thought he had potential in
sports, even though they felt he needed to get stronger. Tae
Kwon Do was an obvious choice as the national sport in
South Korea! He trained with Grandmaster Seung Wan Lee,

and received his 1st Dan in Tae Kwon Do when he was 11 years old. Shortly after that decided to start taking Hap Ki Do, as well, since he wanted to "do something even tougher." He liked it so much that he eventually won the World Hap Ki Do Championship title, in 1974.

Even with all of his training in the martial arts, his biggest aspiration was to take after his father and become a politician – he was student body president in middle and high school, and he actually aspired to become president of South Korea! However, the natural course of his family's events put him in a position where he needed to work to help support and educate his younger siblings. A dream he and his siblings had was to live in the United States, because in global terms, it was much easier to make enough money to support a family, and the education was better, so he and most of the clan moved to North Carolina and Virginia in the 1970s. In 1986, he married his wife, Nan J. Lee, and subsequently had two daughters, Stephanie Lee and Adrian Lee.

In 1986, he decided to open this school to help children and adults in the Triangle through teaching them the disciplines of Tae Kwon Do and Hap Ki Do. He's also been a big proponent of giving back to the community. This has included hosting and sponsoring many events focused on children, including benefits for N.C. Amateur Sports (Raleigh Civic Center, 1992), Make-A-Wish Foundation (1989-2002), and Duke Children's Hospital (2005, 2007). Also, through the years, his generosity and involvement has earned him multiple awards, including "Honorary Mayor of Clinton, NC," "Honorary Citizen of Fayetteville, NC," and "Thanks from Cary."

Master Lee currently holds a 7th Dan in both Tae Kwon Do and Hap Ki Do, and has been internationally active in the use and promotion of these martial arts in the sports and combat arenas. His varied and impressive c.v. includes:

being named to the Tae Kwon Do Hall of Fame by Tae
Kwon Do Times Magazine (Jan 2006);
being featured on the cover of Tae Kwon Do Times
Magazine (Jan 1996);
coordinating the KBS Cup in Seoul, Korea (1994), for
development of TKD in the Olympics;
refereeing for the International World Tae Kwon Do
Federation;
coaching and managing the U.S. National TKD
Junior/Senior Team (1992-1995);
coaching the U.S. National Team at Moscow, Russia (1992)
and Seoul, Korea (1993, 1994)
being named Special Guest of Honor for the European
TKD Championships in St. Petersburg, Russia;
coordinating the TKD Competition in the 1992 North
Carolina State Games;
training U.S. Army troops at Fort Bragg during the first
Gulf War;
acting as a contributing editor for Tae Kwon Do Times
Magazine.
https://www.wta4u.com/videos/CoachLeeCInematicVIde
o_1.mp4

GDE2 is powered by 360WISE and will be broadcast
LIVE for Global audience

GDE2 Mission:
Aggregate fragmented global diaspora Asset/Talents- that
are craving to make Global Impacts & ignite local
Economic Empowerment

Agenda:

(1) Intro of your Hostess 20 years old, gifted, beautiful,
inter-cultural ambassador & unapologetic "Heart of Gold"
- Ms. Lashai Ben-Salmi by 11 years old Amb. Paulo ben
Salmi & 13 years old Princess yasmine Ben Salmi (UK)

PHASE 1:

(1) Introductions of invited guests & US Dept of Commerce Invitation to African Universities

(2) Human Capital Optimixation & Situational Awareness by Col (Rtd) Brian Searcy-(USAF) Chairman BOD US Africa Chamber of commerce & CEO Paratus Group

(3) Revelations: Asset of Papa's Land

(4) Summation by HE Amb (Retd) Robert Perry

PHASE 2: Sharing of Deliverables by:

(1) 360WISE - Global Trend-Setter - "what is local is global"
(2) Borg Invest deals- Guinea, DRC
(3) Congrats to Borg University Consultants John & Sedelle (Trinidad & Tobago)
(4) Legacy 2021 "Flight of Hope"-Above & Beyond Project by Capt Lola- 1st African/British minority to navigate solo around the world in 2017
(5) Legendary SoulJah Kingdom Rise (Aqua Blue Games) by "General Saint" Winston Hislop
(6) Closing Remarks by 6 years old "Mr Intelligent" "Master of Affirmation", Writer, youngest ever STEM Ambassador for Brunel University, Public speaker and co-founder of www.SARVA.net Ambassador with 2021 Mission to "Put a smile on 1 million people" Amire Ben Salmi.

"Think, Act, Grow & Sustain Wealth- Mama Africa" Sir joe
"Imagine the Possibilities from the Mountain Top" Dr, Bailey/Mr. Alexander
"Resistance is Futile" Dr. Onochie

Join HE Bob Perry, Dr, Bailey of Borg Global, Kris of One&Done (UK) Brian Searcy Col (Rtd) USAF, Capt Lola(UK), Capt Terry Grant (Bahamas)Dr. Debbie Bartlett of CEO Network & Economic Emancipation-(Bahamas),

Dr. Onochie, Dr, Val Ozigbo (USA) Okey Bakasi (Nigerian entertainer), Comedian Aki & Pawpaw, Dr. Baba Adams of California, Hon. Kizito (Iyke merchandise Nig), Mr Robert Alexander CEO of 360WISE Media, Bar/Prof KOK (Nollywood Star), Apostle Jerushia of Vegas, Quintus Mcdonald (Ex NFL), Legends of boxing & Taekwondo, millennial/XYZ generations & VIPs like you plus our global audience on 360WiseMedia to welcome 20 years old phenom co-founder SARVA (UK), writer, public speaker, International cultural ambassador and a young lady with a "heart of gold" your Hostess Lashai Ben Salmi (UK).

Co-hosts: Sir Joe Madu, 11 years old Amb Paulo Ben-Salmi (UK), Kris (UK) & Flamboyant Ms. Briony (Netherlands) & beautiful 13 years old Princess Yasmine Ben Salmi (UK).

Sponsorship contact:
africa@globaldiasporaeconomicempowerment.com

https://mail.google.com/mail/u/0?ui=2&ik=69770b74e0
&attid=0.0&permmsgid=msg-
f:1681388549362644292&th=17557dfa2e2b7544&view=at
t&disp=safe

www.borgglobal.com

AMBASSADORSHIPS

I am proud to be the youngest ever ambassador for Water-to-Go because we help to reduce plastic waste and bring cleaner water to the world.

www.watertogo.eu/partnerships/paolobensalmi

I am proud to be an ambassador for TruChallenge because the platform is super cool and you can complete different challenges and also you can give other people challenge to complete.

www.truchallenge.co.uk

I am proud to be an ambassador for VueBox because the platform is super cool and you can upload your own content to their site.

www.vue.co

HOW THOUGHTS BECOME THINGS MOVIE

I would like to say a huge thanks to Douglas Vermeeren who is the creator of this amazing movie called How Thoughts Become Things and for making these below interviews possible. I am so appreciative to Douglas for including mine and my family's names in the credits of this remarkable movie 🎞 🎥:

CALL TO ACTION:

#1 Watch "How Thoughts Become Things" movie now:

Bit.ly/HowThoughtsBecomeThingsMovie2020

#2 Join our affiliate team to help us spread the word for about How Thoughts Become Things Movie:

Bit.ly/HowThoughtsBecomeThingsAffiliateProgram

#1 Watch the full interview on YouTube:
https://youtu.be/MQmB-6CuWc0

#2 Listen to the full interview on my Podcast Show: https://embed.sounder.fm/play/29252?player_style= blue

#1 Watch the full interview on YouTube: https://youtu.be/ldRoXPk1fA4

#2 Listen to the full interview on my Podcast Show: https://life-according-to-paolo.sounder.fm/episode/episode-26-movie-interview-how-thoughts-become

#1 Watch the full interview on YouTube:
https://youtu.be/Ex8x_0JhSAo

#2 Listen to the full interview on my Podcast Show:
https://embed.sounder.fm/play/29252?player_style=blue

ME & MY SIBLINGS

Me and my siblings have a host of products and services that we have designed to empower you to touch the hearts and minds of others for generations to come. Please do not hesitate to get in touch to plant a seed for your future

NEXT GENERATION EDUCATION
Next generation education, turning learners into leaders.

I am so proud about creating SARVA May - November 2020
and co-creating it with my mum, Lashai, Tray-Sean,
Yasmine, Amire and Daniel Barahona.

BONUS CHAPTER WRITTERN BY 11-YEAR-OLD LILY NASH

The acrostic poem of **FORGIVENESS**:

F - For everything we do in the wrong we

O - Owe it to the ones we did it to. Being

R - Righteous isn't about being a know all but to

G - Give some of your knowledge to others

I - If someone has been in the wrong and owe it to me

V - Very much would I like to shout about it but instead

E - Every other part of me wants to forgive them

N - Not what I say: but what God says through me

E - Even if you have an arch nemesis,

S - Say to them that you love them.

S - Say I live for my God, and you should too.

The acrostic poem for **MERCY**:

M - Mercy Is where

E - Everyone has done something wrong in their life

R - Right people will give mercy,

C - Compassion towards others when they could punish.

Y - You should do that too.

Synopsis:

Are mercy and forgiveness the same thing. No Forgiveness is where you have forgiven someone for what they have done wrong. And mercy is where you could punish someone for what they have done. This is my understanding of Mercy and Forgiveness.

Printed in Great Britain
by Amazon

59440614R00078